DBT for Everyone

DBT for EVERYONE

A Guide to the Perks, Pitfalls, and
Possibilities of DBT for Better Mental Health

Kate Sherman and
Michelle Henderson

Jessica Kingsley Publishers
London and Philadelphia

First published in Great Britain in 2024 by Jessica Kingsley Publishers
An imprint of John Murray Press

1

Copyright © Kate Sherman and Michelle Henderson 2024

The right of Kate Sherman and Michelle Henderson to be identified as the Authors of the Work
has been asserted by them in accordance with the Copyright, Designs and Patents Act 1988.

Quotes on pages 86, 92, 93, 95, 101, 130, 131, 141, 165, and 166 are reproduced
from Linehan, M.M. (2015) *DBT Skills Training Handouts and Worksheets.*
New York: The Guilford Press with permission of Guilford Press.

The information contained in this book is not intended to replace the services of trained medical
professionals or to be a substitute for medical advice. You are advised to consult a doctor on any matters
relating to your health, and in particular on any matters that may require diagnosis or medical attention.

Content warning: This book mentions: alcohol, anxiety, panic attacks, blood, depression, drugs, drugging,
addiction, eating disorder, disordered eating, loss of a loved one, death of a parent, death of a loved
one, grief, pregnancy, abortion, miscarriage, self-harm, scars, suicidal thoughts, cancer, trauma, PTSD.

A CIP catalogue record for this title is available from the British Library and the Library of Congress

ISBN 978 1 83997 588 2
eISBN 978 1 83997 589 9

Printed and bound in the United States by Integrated Books International

Jessica Kingsley Publishers' policy is to use papers that are natural, renewable and recyclable
products and made from wood grown in sustainable forests. The logging and manufacturing
processes are expected to conform to the environmental regulations of the country of origin.

Jessica Kingsley Publishers
Carmelite House
50 Victoria Embankment
London EC4Y 0DZ

www.jkp.com

John Murray Press
Part of Hodder & Stoughton Limited
An Hachette UK Company

To my professor Jerry Saltzman (the only reason I finished grad school), and also to my clients, our listeners, and you.

K.S.

To Adam and Noah, for giving me the greatest gifts I could ever ask for, and to my clients (past and present) for teaching me more about healing and growth than any book ever could.

M.H.

Contents

PART 3: EMOTION REGULATION

PART 4: INTERPERSONAL EFFECTIVENESS

Michelle's Preface

Dialectical behavior therapy (DBT) was not designed for someone like me. DBT was created for people who hurt themselves and have anger outbursts. DBT was made for those who have "poor impulse control" and "addictive behaviors." I've never self-harmed in my life, and the thought of yelling at someone or throwing something when I'm angry makes my heart beat faster with trepidation. I don't do anything in my life impulsively, thinking every choice through at length before I act. So how do I find myself writing a book about DBT? What is it about DBT that appeals to me and works for me?

I first came to DBT in 2011 when I worked at a group home. I was fresh out of college with my bachelor's degree in psychology and excited to find some work in my field. So I took a job at a group home, making $10 an hour, working with girls who were suicidal, sexually aggressive, and physically assaultive. These girls had been kicked out of foster homes over and over again, and if I told you their stories your heart would break. These girls had been through some serious shit. Once a week, all six of them piled into a minivan and we went to a two-hour DBT group. This became the night of work I looked forward to the most. I had never heard of DBT before, and I was fascinated. It was something concrete and tangible to do, and I was a sucker for a good worksheet. I learned the skills right along with them and helped them with their homework. I led them in mindfulness activities before dinner as part of their DBT practice and started to understand the skills pretty well. But once I enrolled in graduate school a year later, I stopped working at the group home and put DBT out of my mind. I wouldn't return to it until I did my internship a couple years later. The agency that took me on for my internship (where I would eventually get hired and work with my co-author Kate) wanted to reboot their DBT program, and I was an intern with time on my hands and hours of requirements to fulfill. So, I started leading groups. Now I find myself years later still leading groups and loving it.

But what about...me? Sure, I learned about DBT and I teach DBT, but according to many, I am not "bad enough" to actually *need* DBT skills. There is still a major stereotype that exists about who DBT is meant for, and it isn't me. I am a perfectionist and have a strong Type A personality. I run my own business and have a happy, healthy marriage. But for those of you who are like me, you know there is a lot going on underneath the surface when you function this well. Your brain never quits. You're constantly second-guessing and criticizing yourself. You crave structure in order to feel like you have control over your world, but you also hate how rigid you've become. Just because you're not breaking down on the outside doesn't mean you're not struggling intensely to keep up. And you know what? DBT can help. Mindfulness is absolutely essential to having any kind of balance in life instead of constantly checking things off a to-do list. When life throws a curveball at you, distress tolerance skills provide much-needed guidance to cope instead of trying to control or fix it (as I'm prone to doing). While you may be very good at keeping your emotions in check and not losing your shit, emotion regulation can truly be a godsend in helping you notice *what* you're feeling in the first place. And though you may have overall healthy relationships in your life, if you're afraid to rock the boat and actually talk about your needs, interpersonal effectiveness has you covered. So yes; DBT is for us, too. DBT has changed my life. It has helped me slow down, be more flexible, and become authentic. My hope is that you will be kind to yourself as you learn and practice DBT. You will not do it all perfectly, and you don't need to. I am proud of you for taking this step towards true self-care.

Kate's Preface

Unlike Michelle, DBT *was* designed for someone like me. When I was 19 years old, I stood in a puddle of blood in my bathroom after a particularly bad bout of self-harm. Looking at myself in the mirror, I thought, "If I don't get help, I'm going to accidentally kill myself." That moment was the beginning of my personal journey with DBT. Shortly after that day, I started treatment at what was then the DBT Center of Seattle. It was a "gold standard" DBT program, so I attended a two-hour group every week as well as weekly sessions with an individual DBT therapist. The group portion was a nine-month commitment. I think I worked with that DBT therapist for about an additional year before moving on. It was, quite literally, a life-changing experience. I'm not exaggerating at all when I say I believe DBT saved my life. I learned skills to help me tolerate and moderate my own emotions better. I discovered ways to ground myself back into the here and now, and back to what was real. I was given tools to help me set better boundaries and have healthier relationships.

Despite the monumental impact it had on me, I didn't think much about DBT for many years after I went through the program. Most of the skills had become something I knew and used but rarely thought of in explicit DBT language. I didn't even think of it much while going through school for counseling psychology, where I was reminded of it in classes and textbooks. Then I started work in community mental health and met Michelle. Shortly after we met, we started leading groups together. This reignited in me a passion for these skills. Teaching DBT skills to others, and seeing them have the impact on their lives that they had on my life so many years ago, was incredibly fulfilling. That time was also the start of a relationship that now plays a central role in my personal and professional life. What began as a tentative colleague relationship grew into a treasured friendship, six years and counting of leading groups together, two podcasts, and now...this book.

While no book could possibly replace the immersive experience of a full-fledged DBT program or skills group, my hope for this book is the same hope I have for the members of every group we lead or the listeners of every podcast we release: that it helps make someone's life better and helps you, dear reader, live with more ease. I hope my experience not only as a teacher of DBT, but as a previous student, will help me present the skills in an accessible and intuitive fashion. I hope you learn skills here to help you through the dark times and find healthier ways to take care of yourself. I hope you find in DBT some measure of what I found: a set of skills that changed my life for the better.

Introduction

While our personal histories with DBT started within the past two decades, DBT itself is much older. DBT was developed in the 1970s at the University of Washington in Seattle by Dr. Marsha Linehan, a clinical psychologist. She created DBT originally to treat borderline personality disorder (BPD), a disorder at the time that was considered untreatable by many in the psychology community (Carey 2011). Since its creation, innumerable research studies have been done on DBT, and it has been found to be effective for a wide array of issues beyond BPD (May, Richardi and Barth 2016). DBT programs are structured around four modules with accompanying worksheets to complete. We formatted our book similarly, into four parts corresponding with each of the four DBT modules. The most common worksheets used (and the ones we reference in this book) were created by Linehan herself (2015).

Besides very different personal introductions to DBT as we mentioned in our prefaces, there are a lot of ways in which we differ from each other. Kate walks barefoot everywhere (including in public). Michelle wasn't allowed outside without shoes as a child and so is rarely ever barefoot. Kate dyes her hair myriad colors; Michelle has never dyed her hair. While Michelle is organized and scheduled, Kate is more scattered and impulsive. The list could go on. When we first met in community mental health, we didn't think we would ever become close friends, let alone go on to start two podcasts together and write this book! We've come to see over the years that our differences actually make us a perfect fit as colleagues and friends. DBT is all about dialectics, and the dialectic for the two of us is that we are very different *and* also very similar in meaningful ways. We both are quite talkative while also being attentive listeners (no surprise we became therapists). We've experienced challenging relationships and found understanding in each other. We hold very similar values.

When we were approached to write this book we both thought, "Why us?" After all, there are DBT books already on the market. What could we add to the mix? But the answer came to us almost immediately: we have our different personalities and experiences to share. Neither of us thought when we launched our podcast (*DBT and Me*) that it would grow as much as it has. People benefit from learning the skills, sure, but what we hear repeatedly is how much people benefit from our personal sharing and our dynamic together as we talk about DBT. We have *fun* while we do it, we *laugh* while we do it, and for us, it hardly ever feels like work. A big thing we have in common is that we genuinely enjoy teaching these skills to other people and using them ourselves. *That's* what we hope to bring to this book.

There are a number of different ways you may want to approach the material presented here. If this is your first exposure to the skills, we highly recommend that you read the book through, start to finish, in the order presented. That said, if you know you really need distress tolerance skills, or perhaps your therapist has suggested you look into a particular set of skills, you can skip around in the book, reading it in the order that feels most relevant to you. After you've read through all the skills (or if you're coming to this book for more of a refresher after already going through a DBT course), you can use the index to look up a skill you're struggling with or to find a skill you're wanting to utilize. Ultimately, approach it as it feels and works best for you.

In each chapter you'll hear both of our unique perspectives. After you read about what the skill is, you'll see tips from us both. We will then talk about potential pitfalls of the skill and potential benefits of using it. We end each chapter with questions for you to answer about how you see that skill fitting into your life. Above all, we want you to actually integrate what you're reading by going out and using these skills. We both believe wholeheartedly that DBT is not perfect, *and* it can be extremely helpful and life changing. We think DBT is here for everyone, no matter how big or small your life challenges are. We are grateful for you joining us, and we are honored to be a part of your mental health journey.

PART 1

MINDFULNESS

Mindfulness skills help you stay present, enjoy your day-to-day life, and make choices that better serve your well-being. Mindfulness is foundational for DBT and woven into all of the different modules.

Chapter 1

WISE MIND

Reason Mind/Emotion Mind

ABOUT THIS SKILL

We believe wholeheartedly that wise mind is one of the most important skills to learn and also one of the most difficult to practice consistently. That is why wise mind is the first skill we teach in every group, and it's the first skill we're talking about here in this book. Learning how to access wise mind takes continual effort. Even though it's not easy to use wise mind, when you are able to enter a wise-mind state, the results can be life changing.

Human beings have different areas of the brain that manage decision-making. There is a part (the frontal lobe) that is more focused on "reason" (i.e. logic, organization, objectivity, etc.) and a part (the amygdala) that is focused on "emotion" (i.e. creativity, intuition, subjectivity, etc.). There are strengths and weaknesses to both. The "reason" part (also called "reasonable" or "rational" mind) does a good job of helping you accomplish tasks and think about potential consequences before taking action, while the "emotion" part helps you form relationships with others through giving and receiving emotional expression (Nielsen et al. 2013). You need both in your life and will run into challenges when you rely too much on one side over the other. If you err too much on the reason side, you will become too focused on your goals, proving you are right, and getting things done at the expense of neglecting your own needs and those you care about. If you go too far to the emotion side, you may behave impulsively and sometimes say or do things that hurt other people or get you into trouble because you didn't think first. We believe everyone is prone to falling more to one side or the other when it comes to processing information and making choices.

When "reason" mind and "emotion" mind come together, the blending of the two is called "wise" mind. Wise mind takes the best qualities of both sides and brings them together. Some people describe their wise mind as a feeling of being in touch with a higher power or higher self. Some people think of it as an inner knowing or a powerful, strong intuition about what feels right for them. Oftentimes when people find their wise mind, they experience a sense of relief or a feeling of peace come over them. Being in a wise-mind state is going to look different for everyone, but we hope you find yourself feeling balanced, present, and at ease when you're able to access both your emotional and reasonable parts at the same time. We all have wisdom inside us waiting to be accessed.

KATE'S TIPS

Wise mind is an essential part of DBT, and it's also one of my favorites. Thinking back to when I was a client in a DBT program, I remember being asked questions every week like, "Were you in your wise mind?" or "What would your wise mind say?" Of all the skills, I think wise mind was brought up the most consistently. As you continue your journey through this book, and through the rest of the skills, I hope you will keep this skill at the forefront of your mind. It makes just about every other skill easier and more effective.

Emotion mind

Personally, I spend most of my life in emotion mind. At its most mild, this may look like following my heart a little more than my head. At its most helpful/positive, this looks like showing up for my clients with compassion, empathy, and warmth. At its worst or most destructive, this looks like self-harm, throwing things, and other forms of lashing out or falling apart. I hope this demonstrates that emotion mind is far from being all bad. Emotion mind can encompass a lot of love, passion, and creativity. Our culture is prone to belittling emotion mind, seeing it as associated with femininity and therefore as lesser and weak. This is simply inaccurate or, at the very least, incomplete. While there is destructive potential in emotion mind, there's also a tremendous capacity for creation.

Reason mind

While I am often led by my heart, there are activities and events that require me to lean more heavily on my reason mind. If I'm trying to hang drywall, work my way through a math problem, or learn how to repair a piece of electronics, I want to be in my reason mind. Just like emotion mind, reason mind can look very different at different times. It can range from keeping a cool head in an emergency to being coldly logical and withdrawn emotionally from a partner. Just as I said that emotion mind isn't all bad, I'd like to fight societal bias by saying reason mind isn't all good. Logic is associated with masculinity in our culture and considered superior. However, there are places, times, and situations where you need your emotions to show up, and where being only logical will damage you and your relationships.

Wise mind

One of the main questions we get when we run DBT groups is, "How do I find wise mind?" For me, wise mind is all about a feeling. No matter what emotions I'm going through at the time, when I make a wise-mind decision, there's a sense of a weight being lifted, of peace, of *rightness*. I may be angry, or grieving, or a hundred other things, but through it all sings this sense of rightness. I then remember what this rightness feels like in my body, so I can also tell when I'm not in my wise mind; it simply won't feel *right*. This is more about big decisions than everyday choices, but the same kind of sensation is there even for the smaller stuff; it's just more subdued. For the smaller choices, I really have to get quiet and listen to myself to feel that sense of rightness. Nevertheless, if the choice I'm making aligns with my wise mind, that sensation is there. It is in looking for that feeling that I'm most able to find and get into my wise mind.

MICHELLE'S TIPS

Understanding wise mind and being able to find it are two different things. For many years when I led DBT groups, I taught what wise mind was, but I didn't really talk about how to get there because I didn't know myself. It was only through my own work in therapy and my therapist helping me cultivate the idea of a "wise adult self" that I came to know my own wise mind.

Emotion mind

When we boil it down, our emotion mind is all about what we feel. I prioritize and value my emotions highly. I'm an avid journaler, getting everything I think and feel out onto the page when I write. I am also an external processor, meaning I want to verbalize what I'm feeling. Maybe it comes from Cancer being my astrological sign, but I live in a world where I spend a considerable amount of time talking about and being with my emotions. When I'm in my emotion mind too much, I get preoccupied with how strongly I'm feeling my emotions, and it can be hard for me to take a break from thinking about painful emotional experiences. If you're like me, it's incredibly important to not only have an outlet for your emotions (like a journal or trusted friend), but to also know when to take a break from thinking about what's causing you emotional distress.

Reason mind

My reason mind looks very much like doing mind (which will be discussed in the next chapter). Organization and to-do lists feel like breathing to me. I can be very persistent, and I work at things until they are complete (often to my detriment). I'm also quite analytical and like to know the rationale behind decisions and why people do what they do. When I am too much in my reason mind, I become solely focused on the task or issue in front of me, and I neglect to pause and check in with myself about my needs. I have found it necessary to build in breaks, just like with emotion mind.

Wise mind

I am in my wise mind when I pause. When I'm there, I ask myself, "What do I need?" and "Is this serving me?" Those questions help me tap into self-care and make decisions that honor my emotional experience and slow me down when I'm trying to get too much done at once. Here are my favorite strategies when it comes to finding your wise mind.

Tip 1: Find your wise adult self

Think about a time when you made a decision that served you and was beneficial for your life. This may be a big decision (like a career change or leaving an unhealthy relationship) or a small decision (deciding to take a walk or talk to a friend). As you think about these things, imagine who you were when you made that choice. What age were you? How did you look? What were your thoughts and emotions at the time?

When you're able to pause and reflect on past wise-mind decisions you've made, you're creating a relationship with the part of you that made those choices. You can think of that part as your wise adult, and you can return to thinking about this part when you're facing challenging decisions in the future. Because I have worked on this extensively with my own therapist, she will often say to me in sessions to close my eyes and imagine my wise adult. I then pause and listen to what my wise adult says about a situation and find clarity.

Tip 2: Ask what someone else would do

If it's too difficult for you to think about wise-mind decisions you've made in the past, think about someone you believe embodies the traits of wise mind. This could be someone you know or a fictional character. This person could be living or dead. Imagine them standing before you and have a dialogue with them about what you're struggling with; ask them questions and see what answers you receive. Think about what they would do or what guidance they could provide.

Tip 3: Find a mantra

Having a go-to phrase can really help with finding wise mind. For me, I commonly will say, "Let it be" (or I'll listen to the song by The Beatles, and it nearly always does the trick to bring me to my wise mind). You can even just pick a singular word such as "patience," "trust," "acceptance," or "pause." If you repeat your mantra or word enough (especially if you take an intentional breath as you do so), you'll notice a shift in how your body is feeling physically, and this will likely change your thinking to a more wise-mind direction.

PITFALLS
Pitfall 1

One of the most common mistakes folks make is **thinking that wise mind is equal parts emotion mind and reason mind**. While this may be true some of the time, it's certainly not necessary. Different situations are going to call for being more in your emotion mind or your reason mind. Because a part of wise mind is being effective, make sure you're leaning more towards whichever side the situation requires. Just because we use the word "balanced" to describe wise mind does not mean it's a balance composed of equal parts. It's more like the balance of someone walking a high wire. In order to keep their balance, they sometimes need to lean more one way or more the other; that's the kind of balance we're talking about when we describe wise mind.

Pitfall 2

Another common misconception about wise mind is **believing the goal is to be in your wise mind all day, every day**. While that would probably feel pretty good, we strongly believe it's an unattainable goal. It sets the bar far too high, and guarantees you'll be failing far more than you succeed. Rather than living in your wise mind 24/7, start by setting the bar at being in your wise mind at least once a week, or maybe once a day. Set the bar somewhere you can reach it. Humans are far more motivated by success than by failure, so set yourself up to succeed. It'll keep you coming back to your wise mind, rather than causing you to avoid it because you associate it with feelings of failure or shame.

Pitfall 3

People often believe that a wise-mind decision will always feel good, comfortable, or easy. Sadly, this just isn't true. Nearly everyone has been in a situation where the "right" (or wise-mind) decision was terrifying and/or painful. For instance, you might know that ending your long-term relationship is the wise-mind thing to do, but that doesn't mean it won't be painful and frightening to leave. While it's common to find a sense of peace when reaching a wise-mind decision, that peace doesn't eradicate every other uncomfortable feeling that may be there. Listen to/ feel for a sense of "rightness," but don't wait to find a choice that's not emotionally difficult. There might not be one.

BENEFITS
Benefit 1

Spending too much time in emotion mind or reason mind leaves you clinging tightly to your experience. Someone in their emotion mind believes strongly that their emotion reflects reality (e.g. "I'm scared of this, therefore it must be dangerous"). Someone in reason mind gets caught up in research, facts, and trying to prove a point. When you are in your wise mind, you let go of the need to prove others wrong or justify yourself. **You may feel settled and calm, seeing the big picture of what you're experiencing in a larger context.** Wise mind is about seeing the entire forest, not just a single tree.

Benefit 2

At its core, anxiety is worry about the future and things you can't control. **Wise mind helps you come back to the present and focus on what you *can* do.** If you're able to pause and notice anxiety early on, getting into your wise mind might prevent a panic attack. It can help you communicate more calmly with those around you because you'll feel calmer yourself.

Benefit 3

Everyone holds some beliefs or commits some actions that don't work very well for them. These may be things you learned from your parents/caregivers in early childhood or things you started doing after experiencing a trauma. Unhealthy coping mechanisms and reactions can take hold of your life and leave you with regrets and shame later on. **Wise mind can break you out of ruts and lead you to change course in your life.** When you're contemplating making a change or you realize something is damaging your life, this is a perfect time to find your wise mind and make a new choice.

EXERCISE

When you think about reason mind/emotion mind, which do you identify with the most? How have you seen this show up in your daily life?

_____

_____

_____

_____

_____

_____

_____

Where do you think you'll struggle most with the concepts of reason mind/ emotion mind?

_____

_____

_____

_____

_____

_____

_____

How can you imagine this skill being useful to you in your life? How can you see yourself implementing it?

_____

_____

_____

_____

_____

_____

_____

_____

_____

Chapter 2

WISE MIND
Doing Mind/Being Mind

ABOUT THIS SKILL

Another way to conceptualize wise mind is to think of it as the intersection between "doing" and "being." Incorporating aspects of both "reason" and "emotion" can be thought of as finding mental and emotional balance with decision-making, whereas practicing both doing and being reflects a balance with how you spend your time and energy.

When you catch yourself doing either "too much" or "not enough," accessing your wise mind is extremely beneficial. If you identify as a procrastinator, you'll benefit from bringing in your "doing" mind. If you are a "work-aholic" or perfectionist, you'll benefit from finding your "being" mind. Wise mind in this context can be especially helpful for people who find themselves lacking direction or motivation due to life circumstances such as sudden unemployment, the onset of an injury/ illness, or feelings of chronic boredom. It can also be helpful for those who are busy balancing multiple roles (i.e. working and attending school, being a working parent, etc.) to help with slowing down.

Finding wise mind with doing and being means finding a state of flow (Csikszentmihalyi 1990). There is action involved and a task being performed (doing mind) and yet, the person is completely present, without concern about when they complete the task or what the end result will be (being mind). Most of the time, you probably find yourself falling too much to one side or the other, either resisting tasks that need to be done or busying yourself with a checklist of things to do. Finding a wise-mind place with doing and being helps you determine what to do with your time and energy. Not only do you know when it is important to "work," but you also know when it is important to "play." Furthermore, sometimes work can feel like play when you are truly in your wise mind, at one with what you are doing, no matter what the activity is.

KATE'S TIPS

Much like reason mind and emotion mind, most people find they skew more towards either doing mind or being mind. I'm much more connected to my doing mind than my being mind. Sometimes, the first thing I'm aware of in the morning is my brain slipping into the future to plan what I need to get done for the day. I can find it difficult to stay in the present and to let go of being goal oriented.

Doing mind

Doing mind is often the state that is seen as superior. After all, doing mind is what helps you get through school, be a good employee, stay organized, manage money, and work towards most goals you have. However, as someone who spends an imbalanced amount of my time in doing mind, I can tell you there are disadvantages as well. Too much time spent in doing mind leaves me very anxious and makes it difficult for me to relax. If you're unsure of how to tune in here, you may notice your own doing mind if you feel a sense of drive, a push to be moving forward, or a sense of being "on track." Then check to see if you're feeling anxious, frantic, overwhelmed, or guilty. We all need our doing minds in order to navigate our lives, especially as adults, but too much will weigh you down and make managing your day-to-day life even more stressful.

Being mind

Being mind is a space where you can contemplate your life and actions, without the urge or obligation to *do* anything. What's the downside, you ask? Well, most of us have shit we need or want to get done. While being mind gives you a break from feeling pressured, it is also a space where you're unlikely to accomplish your goals or move forward. I often find I struggle to consciously access my being mind or allow myself to stay there for very long. The moments I'm most strongly in my being mind are when I'm out in nature. There are times when I literally stop to smell the roses, or when I'm caught up unexpectedly in the beauty of a sunset or landscape. Even though those moments are fleeting, they allow me small sips of time when everything else falls away, and I can simply *be*. Moments like those might also help you find your being mind, and experience what it feels like. Knowing how it feels once will give you a better roadmap for finding it again.

Wise mind

The purpose here is being effective, not being perfectly balanced. I find this state the most readily when I'm tending to my houseplants (or sometimes my garden). I get into a place of flow, where I have goals or objectives I'm working on, but without clinging to the outcomes. If you're struggling to find your wise mind here, start by finding things that you already enjoy, or naturally find yourself in a state of flow when doing. If you have a hobby or activity where you really get into the zone, that's a great place to start with this skill.

MICHELLE'S TIPS

Finding the balance of doing and being can feel like walking the high wire we mentioned in the pitfalls section last chapter, leaning more to one side and then the other as you go. It is completely natural in life to either do "too much doing" or "too much being." What matters is having awareness of the impact it has on you to be in each state and having strategies to make changes if needed.

Doing mind

I live in my doing mind nearly all the time. I grew up watching my mother be in her doing mind, rarely sitting down for a moment (until she would fall asleep on the couch at the end of the day, utterly exhausted). I have a to-do list at all times in my phone, and it dictates my day from start to finish. I often fall into the trap of thinking I will feel better the more I accomplish and check off that list. The result is that I am focused on work far more than I am focused on taking care of myself. Living in my doing mind leaves me feeling accomplished, but it doesn't leave me feeling renewed or refreshed. It's become important for me to get comfortable with things being left unfinished. I have to tell myself repeatedly that things do not have to get done right now when I am too much in my doing mind.

Being mind

When I am in my being mind, it feels like coming up to gasp for air before I go back to getting things done. If I find myself in being mind, it is typically very temporary and fleeting. I used to have about one day a month where I would fully live in my being mind, and it looked like sitting on the couch all day watching TV. I would only do this after having sufficiently checked off a number of things on my to-do list in the days prior, and it didn't leave me feeling as refreshed as I hoped it would. Sometimes I find myself feeling *more* tired when I'm in my being mind. What helps me most is making sure that I am making space for being every single day. I don't always do well at this, but it helps to just be able to take a few minutes to pause. Because I'm a morning person, it's easiest for me to take that time for myself soon after I wake up. If you're more of a night owl, it might come more naturally to make time just before bed.

Wise mind

Because I spend so much time in doing mind, I need to intentionally remind myself to be. It doesn't come naturally to me, but creating space for being *before* doing is the way I find my wise mind, and you can do this too if you often get stuck in doing mind. At the start of a busy day, do something just for you before you embark on your to-do list. If you were thinking about going for a walk after cleaning your house, go for a walk first. Dance around your living room for a little bit before starting a homework assignment. Don't buy into the myth that there isn't enough time. Playing before you start working will actually help you feel better and therefore, you'll get more done when you do start to work.

PITFALLS
Pitfall 1
Trying to access or spend time in your being mind can feel like being lazy and unproductive. Many people see being mind as some sort of treat, or reward: something they'll give themselves once they've accomplished all their tasks. Because of that, it's common to struggle with feeling guilty. **There's so much societal pressure around always *doing* that any time productivity isn't your main focus, it can feel like you're a failure, leading to self-judgment.** If this is something you're struggling with, try to remember you can't be in your wise mind without pulling in at least *some* of your being mind. Being mind isn't some sort of reward either. Rather, it's a necessary component to reaching your wise mind and is no less important than your doing mind. And don't worry if you have to remind yourself of this a lot. You're fighting against years of social programming.

Pitfall 2
For some folks, the idea of their being mind feels like a slippery slope. There can be this worry that, if you enter a being-mind state, you'll just...never leave. Or, at the very least, that you'll struggle to leave or to incorporate more of your doing mind. This is proof that our society puts too much emphasis on doing. If simply being feels that tempting, you're likely not doing enough of it! **If you avoid your being mind too assiduously, then it can almost become a craving of sorts.** This is because everyone needs some being mind in their lives, or they fall out of balance. The more you're afraid you won't leave your being mind, the more you need it. It may seem paradoxical, but deliberately incorporating more being into your life on a regular basis will make getting into your doing mind easier. You know you'll get more "being" time down the line, and so you won't feel the need to cling to it when you allow yourself to go there.

Pitfall 3
Another common struggle is reaching or staying in doing mind. Many of the reasons you might find it difficult to engage with doing mind are fear based. This could look like feelings of inadequacy, helplessness, fear of judgment, or a host of other issues. **When you let fears keep you from taking action, you miss out on huge swaths of your life.** While there is great comfort and even a sense of safety to be found in your being mind, ultimately it is also a place of stagnancy. Comfort is necessary for a healthy and balanced life, but so is growth and achievement, neither of which is possible if you live only in your being mind. If you are someone who has to work at reaching your doing mind, try coming at it from a place of mindful awareness of your emotions. If you can identify your fears from a nonjudgmental space, you can better soothe and move through those fears, instead of letting them keep you stuck.

BENEFITS
Benefit 1
Being in a wise-mind state of both doing and being increases enjoyment of activities. Think about this with eating: do you enjoy your food more when you eat slowly and savor every bite or when you're shoveling food in as quickly as possible? We live in a world where we tend to feel very rushed. We're so worried about arriving somewhere late that we forget to enjoy the drive to get there. We wake up in the morning and don't take time to pause before we start moving to get ready to leave the house. **Slowing down often leads to paying attention in a new way to what you're doing, and that can make you appreciate what you're doing more.**

Benefit 2
As was mentioned in the pitfalls section, research has shown that **you actually accomplish more when you allow yourself to take more breaks and just be.** One example of this is recognizing that employees are more productive working four days a week instead of five (Barnes 2020). How can this be when they are working fewer hours? Because the balance between work and life is better. They have more time to "be" outside of work, so they are more refreshed when they do come into work to start "doing." Working *more* rarely results in working more *effectively* and can lead to a whole host of issues, including burnout. This means if you have a lot on your plate, one of the best things you can do for yourself is take a break to "be."

Benefit 3
Some people have barriers to being as physically active as they'd like to be due to physical limitations, illness, and more. They can start to feel frustrated by the sedentary nature of their lives, and this can lead to them feeling like they are just "being" without any "doing." **Finding activities that don't require much physical effort still counts as "doing," and our brains benefit from even minimal physical activity** (Omura et al. 2020). Don't put too much pressure on yourself to be active if this is a challenge for you. Even an activity that doesn't involve much (if any) physical exertion, but does require some mental effort, can be the perfect balance of keeping an active "doing" mind with a "being" body.

EXERCISE

Does thinking of doing mind/being mind speak to you more or less than emotion mind/reason mind? Why or why not?

_____

_____

_____

_____

_____

_____

_____

What do you think will be hardest for you when it comes to doing mind/ being mind?

_____

_____

_____

_____

_____

_____

_____

Where can you imagine this concept being useful to you in your life? How can you see yourself implementing it?

_____

_____

_____

_____

_____

_____

_____

_____

_____

Chapter 3

THE "WHAT" COMPONENTS OF MINDFULNESS

Jon Kabat-Zinn, the founder of Mindfulness-Based Stress Reduction, defines mindfulness as "paying attention in a particular way: on purpose, in the present moment, and nonjudgmentally" (Kabat-Zinn 1994, p.4). You will notice that "sitting still" and "silence" are not part of this definition. If you think the only way to practice mindfulness is to sit down, close your eyes, and meditate, you are incorrect. Mindfulness can be practiced in a variety of ways, both formally and informally. Formal mindfulness practices involve stopping other activities in your life and "doing" mindfulness. This could mean attending a yoga class, meditating, or engaging in prayer or other spiritual practices. Informal mindfulness is what we are going to be talking about as we describe the first three mindfulness skills of DBT (the other three will be discussed in the next chapter). Informal mindfulness is paying attention on purpose, like Kabat-Zinn says. Paying attention in this specific way can be done anytime, anywhere, with any activity you're doing.

Increasing our awareness so we move through the world more mindfully is no small feat; we run on autopilot *a lot* as we go through our days. You typically don't need to pay much attention when doing tasks like brushing your teeth, drinking coffee, or getting dressed because these are activities you've done thousands of times. On the one hand, this makes sense, and on the other hand, it results in missing out on fully experiencing things as much as you could. Your brain starts to multitask while you're doing those easier tasks, and before you know it, your mind is somewhere else (i.e. making the grocery list, thinking about weekend plans, reflecting on an argument with a partner, etc.).

There are benefits to living more mindfully (and drawbacks to multitasking) which we will discuss later in this chapter. For now, let's talk about the three components of mindfulness that help with paying attention on purpose, in the present moment.

THE THREE "WHATS" OF MINDFULNESS

Observe

Observation is about much more than just seeing with our eyes what is going on around us. We observe the world through all five of our senses, taking in touch, sounds, sights, smells, and tastes, often all at once. When it comes to mindfulness, you must first be aware of how you're experiencing the world through your senses. You can choose to observe and focus on just about anything in the environment around you or on your own inner experience, including physical sensations, emotions, or thoughts arising in you. Observing through the five senses is important for maintaining a nonjudgmental stance (a concept that will be discussed in the next chapter). Observation requires you to focus on what is in the present moment, just as you are noticing it right now. You can't observe something that has already happened in the past, nor can you observe something that has yet to happen in the future. All you can do is take in what's happening right here and now, and pay attention.

Describe

Our minds are constantly at work putting words to the experiences we are having. We never truly stop thinking, and most people think in the form of language. The words we use to describe what we're experiencing are extremely important, as our thoughts have a direct influence on our emotions, which then influence our actions. When practicing mindfulness, you want to describe just what you are observing right then. Words often will come up without intentional effort as you pay attention. What does take intentional effort is ensuring that you are describing things as objectively as possible, focusing on the reality of the current moment, without coloring it with your opinions. For example, if you are trying a new food for the first time that has an unfamiliar smell, instead of describing the smell as "gross," you might tell yourself, "This is a new smell I've never experienced before." Instead of saying, "The weather sucks today," you can say, "It's raining outside."

Participate

Because mindfulness encompasses much more than just meditation, it is possible to be mindful of any activity you're doing. You have the choice to intentionally observe and describe anything that's happening at any moment. Once you're observing and describing something, you can then actively participate with it. This means focusing your entire energy on that thing. After all, we are all doing *something* at all times, even if that something is just breathing, walking, or sitting. Instead of having your mind be elsewhere, pay attention to your five senses and observe how it feels to be doing the activity. If you find your thoughts focusing on something else, try to describe and focus your thoughts on the activity as much as possible. Be fully present with what you're doing, focusing all your physical energy on it.

KATE'S TIPS

Mindfulness is my jam. I'm in love with the neuroscience behind it, and I love how big an impact just a little mindfulness can have. I consistently have clients tell me how much it improves their day to just add in a few minutes of mindfulness. I love the flexibility and adaptability of mindfulness as well as its accessibility.

Observe

Observing is ideally just about noticing without words...which is a problem for me. As someone with aphantasia (the inability to see images in your mind), most of the instructions given for observing are impossible for me. I cannot watch my thoughts, and I find it almost impossible to notice anything in the outside world without words cropping up either. If you struggle with this step like I do, I recommend starting with observing your own body and physical sensations. When I'm wanting to practice observe, I always start with noticing my body. Whether it's noticing the churn of anxiety in my gut or just the smell of rain in the air, quieting my mind to better tune into my body is my best way to sink into observe without turning to words.

Describe

I like this aspect of mindfulness because I'm a word person, and this is where you get to add words in! The most important aspect of this skill, to my way of thinking, is making sure you're keeping your descriptions nonjudgmental, sticking to just the observable facts. Whether this be your thoughts, your bodily sensations, or the world around you, you want to be as neutral as possible. As a person who is prone to flowery, poetic language and hyperbole, this is sometimes a big ask of myself! One way I work on this aspect of the skill is revision. If I'm observing the smell of rain in the air, for instance, my thoughts may first sound like "I'm smelling the most amazing, delicious smell of rain on the air." It sometimes isn't until I "hear" myself having the thought that I notice the judgments (which can be even harder when you are judging something positively). So, then I would try the thought again: "I'm smelling the rain on the air." Ta-da! A nonjudgmental description. While this was a simple thought and so simply fixed, you may need more than one revision for more complicated observations.

Participate

When you lean into this skill, you'll notice your mind and your emotions quiet down. It doesn't allow space for ruminations, emotional spirals, or future tripping. As someone prone to all three, this is why I appreciate this element of mindfulness so much. While it makes sense to approach participate by turning to activities you already thoroughly enjoy, I prefer to tackle it from a different direction. I practice participating in situations that range from the daily banalities to the actually oner-ous. It's easy for me to slip into participating when I'm hiking or baking or doing things that already draw me in, but I benefit more from practicing it with things that are routine or which I dislike. For things that are routine, my best tip here is to do it *differently* than you usually do. Wash your body in a different order in the shower, deliberately do a chore in a novel fashion, drink your morning tea while trying to stand on one foot; do whatever changes help you stay grounded to those activities where it is easiest to go on autopilot. Doing unpleasant tasks mindfully may sound terrible, but it honestly makes the experience better. It helps you accomplish it more quickly, with fewer judgments, and with a less unpleasant inner monologue (fewer thoughts about how awful or unfair the thing is). My best trick here is to set a short timer somewhere to go off every minute or few minutes to remind you to return to being mindful of the task. With practice and repetition, it will get easier!

MICHELLE'S TIPS

It first feels important to say that mindfulness takes a lot of work. It's not easy to have your brain be present when there's so much to worry about in the future and so much to think about from the past. We encourage you to start very small with mindfulness; it is an unrealistic expectation to do these three things all the time. If you're able to do any of what I talk about here for even five minutes a day, you're on your way to living a more mindful life!

Observe

While many people practice mindfulness by observing the outside world and what's going on around them, I mostly practice mindfulness of what's going on within me, similarly to Kate. This typically means observing one of two things: I'm either focusing on the physical sensations of how emotions show up in my body or observing my thoughts. Oftentimes when I'm not being mindful, I'm too busy "doing" to pause and notice how I'm actually "feeling." My body tells me what I'm feeling emotionally if I tune in to it. Does my throat feel tight, letting me know I feel nervous to talk to someone? Do I have a pit in my stomach and feel ashamed about something? Without noticing mindfully, I'm going to miss important information about what I'm feeling emotionally. When I can pause even briefly to notice, I'm able to make more wise-mind decisions based on the information I observe from my body. Most of us experience thoughts about the past or the future, and I am no different. Mindfully observing my thoughts brings me back to what is right in front of me and what I'm doing right then. When observing, I encourage you to ask yourself the following questions:

1. What do I notice in my body/what is my body trying to tell me right now?

2. As I observe physical sensations in my body, what emotion am I noticing (anger, sadness, disgust, joy, or fear)?

3. What am I thinking right now? Is this a future-focused thought or a past-focused thought? What present-moment thought can I focus on instead?

Describe

I use two different self-talk strategies when describing my current experience. The first is to talk out loud to myself. You might think that only "crazy people" do that, but talking out loud to yourself can help you process information differently (Kirkham, Breeze and Mari-Beffa 2012). Practice describing what you're thinking, feeling or doing out loud (as nonjudgmentally as you can). Another way I utilize describe is by talking to myself (either silently or aloud) about each step I'm doing as I do an activity. This can be especially helpful if the task feels big, overwhelming, or if it's something you've never done before. As cliche as this sounds, take it one step at a time and narrate everything as you're doing it. This is something we often do with young children as we're helping them through a task but forget to do for ourselves as adults. It really helps you pay attention and organize your thoughts.

Participate

My two favorite activities for practicing participating are dancing and journaling. When I dance, I don't think; I just move my body and it gives me the opportunity to notice how that feels and pay attention to the music I'm dancing to. You would be amazed how just listening to one or two songs and dancing along can help you be more present for a few minutes a day. This same idea can be applied to playing a sport or singing. With journaling, you are given an opportunity to put the observations of your thoughts and emotions into writing. The act of writing gives you a chance to participate with that observation of yourself and describe it. Journaling helps me organize what I'm experiencing emotionally and give it a voice.

PITFALLS
Pitfall 1

Throughout our years of teaching DBT, **the most common reason we hear for why people stop practicing mindfulness is because they "aren't good at it."** Clients say their mind wanders almost immediately and they can't stay focused on the present. Our response is to tell clients to meditate badly on purpose. Here's the truth: everyone sucks at mindfulness when they are first learning. The lives we live in this modern world teach our brains to be the opposite of mindful. We're expected to multitask, and we have new data coming in at us all the time. *Of course* your mind wanders right away. No wonder you struggle to stay in the moment! If you manage to stay focused and present for even 30 seconds when you first start practicing, that is a huge win, not a failure. In reality, doing it badly is oftentimes more helpful than doing it well. Think of it like lifting weights. Every rep you do of lifting weights helps to strengthen and condition the muscles you're using, right? The same is true for every time you catch your mind wandering and bring it back to the task at hand. Every time you refocus, you're building the "muscles" in your brain, and working to condition it to a new set of behaviors. This is going to take time, and it's going to take a lot of reps with the proverbial weights. So again: go meditate (or practice mindfulness in whatever way you please) badly. It's good for you.

Pitfall 2

After quitting because they feel they are doing it badly, **the next most common reason folks give for why they aren't practicing mindfulness is because they "don't have enough time."** This is simple to fight against because one of the most awesome things about mindfulness is that you can do it *anytime, anywhere*, about *anything*. You can be mindful of your current outside environment (which is always there), your body (which you are always in), and your thoughts/emotions (which you always have). No matter where you are or what you are doing, you can still be mindful. Mindfulness isn't an activity or action; it's a way of being and a state of mind. It changes how you are experiencing or viewing your reality. While it may be nice to sit and meditate if that's something you enjoy doing, it isn't necessary for the practice of mindfulness. Mindfulness doesn't require a space on your schedule, just some space in your mind.

Pitfall 3

Lastly, people often avoid practicing mindfulness during unpleasant situations or when feeling difficult emotions. Mindfulness creates a space of true awareness. It removes a lot of the buffers you may have between you and your experiences, and that may leave you feeling raw and vulnerable (which may feel uncomfortable). **It can be tempting to only practice mindfulness during times when things are placid or pleasant.** It can also mean focusing solely on pleasant things while deliberately avoiding unpleasant experiences inside or outside yourself. Though it can be painful to be mindful of unpleasant things, this awareness also helps you more accurately label your experience, communicate about your experience to others, and gain insight into why you may be struggling in the moment. Mindfulness also causes you to take a proverbial "step back" from your experience (in order to observe it), which actually makes the unpleasant experience easier to bear. If you notice yourself shying away from awareness of tough situations, see if you can instead lean into the difficult experience. You may be surprised by the benefits.

BENEFITS
Benefit 1

When we are mindful, **we experience greater appreciation of the "little things" in life.** You may have heard the expression "stop and smell the roses," meaning it's important to notice what's around you and pause to take it in. You don't want to miss out on the roses! However, there are so many things to observe in the world, that it's impossible to take in every nuance and detail of what's happening. Just choose *something* to observe. When you make an intentional effort to observe the simple things you do every day and notice how they feel (really savoring that first sip of coffee or closing your eyes while you listen to a song so you hear each note), you might just start appreciating things in a new way (Keng, Smoski and Robins 2011).

Benefit 2

One common way to practice mindfulness is to observe your breath. You don't have to change it; just pay attention to it. When you focus your attention on your breath, it tends to naturally slow down, and you will experience a feeling of calm. As you practice mindfulness, you are paying attention to just what is in the present. Oftentimes our sympathetic nervous system (stress response) gets activated because we're focused on either the future or the past. **Mindfulness pulls you out of rumination and can remind you that you are currently safe.** You can practice mindfulness by telling yourself, "Right now, I am in my house washing the dishes," and this can change your physiology as you remind yourself that the stressful thoughts are not related to the here-and-now (Keng et al. 2011).

Benefit 3

Not only does mindfulness pause rumination and stressful thoughts, but **it also helps with lengthening attention span for tasks** (Zanesco et al. 2018). Every time you practice mindfulness, you are training your mind to focus where you want it to go. If you struggle with feeling like your mind is "all over the place" or like your thoughts are "racing," turning to mindfulness is the key to slowing down your brain and recentering on what is right in front of you. When you can do this, you'll likely complete the task faster and more accurately than if your mind was wandering during it. If your mind starts to wander, return to observing and describing exactly what's happening in front of you, over and over, so you'll be able to participate fully while you do the task.

EXERCISE

Which of the "what" skills do you think will come most naturally to you, and why?

Which of the "what" skills do you think you'll struggle with implementing, and why?

What's one way you can start practicing the "what" skills in your daily life?

Chapter 4

THE "HOW" COMPONENTS OF MINDFULNESS

Remember Jon Kabat-Zinn's definition of mindfulness from the last chapter? He defines mindfulness as "paying attention in a particular way: on purpose, in the present moment, and nonjudgmentally" (Kabat-Zinn 1994, p.4). It's not enough to observe, describe, and participate with our surroundings and ourselves. It is crucial to do those three things in a specific way: nonjudgmentally, one-mindfully, and effectively. To be clear, incorporating these three "how" aspects of mindfulness into your life is tough. It takes a lot of practice to make sure you're observing, describing, and participating in this fashion.

THE THREE "HOWS" OF MINDFULNESS
Nonjudgmentally
The word "judgment" has a bad reputation. When we typically think about "judging" someone, we believe that means we're negatively evaluating them and finding all of their flaws. In reality, judgments can be positive or negative and are simply opinions. Judgments help you make immediate decisions and can even be lifesaving (if you judge a situation as unsafe and avoid it). When it comes to mindfulness, however, your judgments can get you into trouble. Our brains are designed to "tell us stories" and "fill in the blanks" when we don't know information (Burton 2019). Sometimes our mind judges something, and we believe that judgment is true when it may not be. Let's say you do not like spicy food; you've tried spicy food a number of times and determined it's not for you. When a friend asks you to try a new food for the first time and tells you it may be spicy, you may make an instant judgment that you likely won't enjoy the food based on past experience. A more mindful way to think of this situation would be to tell yourself you don't know what the food tastes like yet and to be present to this tasting experience rather than comparing it to past experiences.

If you judge something positively, you may be more likely to overlook other options. Let's say you work with three people: one person you like strongly, one person you feel neutral towards, and one person you dislike. When your boss asks you to pick someone to work on a project with, you'd likely pick the person you already like. If you were to pause and practice mindfulness, you might try to access your wise mind and evaluate who might be best suited to the project based on what you have factually observed. This might involve letting go of prior judgments of your co-workers and assumptions you may have made in the past about them. It's natural and normal for you to have likes and dislikes, preferences and opinions. This is part of being human. What's important is to notice when those judgments impact your decision-making in a way that does not serve you.

Your judgments can stop you from having new experiences (such as deciding you already dislike a food before trying it) and from acting effectively (such as deciding you don't want to work with a co-worker who could be the best person for the job). When you describe things just as they are in a nonjudgmental way, you are more likely to be open to what reality is presenting to you without turning away from it or experiencing willfulness.

One-mindfully

One-mindfully is a difficult part of practicing mindfulness because we don't typically do things "one at a time." We're checking our phones while drinking our morning coffee, while having the TV on in the background, while also thinking about what we need to do for the day. To practice mindfulness one-mindfully is exactly as it sounds: it's doing one thing at a time. When you're watching a movie, don't look at your phone or fold laundry or do anything else during it; be one with the experience of watching the movie. When you're eating, actually taste your food and focus on the task of eating without being distracted by other things. You may be already thinking that this won't work for your lifestyle because there's too much to do. This is why it's an unrealistic expectation to think you can practice mindfulness all day long; we know modern lives are not designed for this. If you find even just a single minute (literally, 60 seconds) of your day to do just one thing, give that a try. Perhaps it's when you first wake up in the morning or just before you go to bed. Doing something (anything) one-mindfully gives your brain a much-needed break from the multitasking it's doing all day long. If your mind starts to wander, come back to the basics of observing and describing what your senses are experiencing in that moment.

Effectively

Doing things effectively means doing what works. It's listed as the sixth mindfulness component for a reason; you must be doing all five of the other things already discussed in order to be effective. When you do things mindlessly, you often get into ruts. You may develop reflexive ways of communicating with other people that are abrasive or find you keep going with a task instead of taking a break when it would benefit you. When you practice mindfulness, you see new possibilities. You're noticing your world in a different, more intentional, purposeful sort of way, and you're letting go of judgments and multitasking. This means you might discover new, more effective pathways, especially with communication. You communicate more effectively if you're truly present to a conversation with someone else and open to doing what will work for both of you instead of just what will work for you. When you're effective, you're able to see patterns of communication for what they are and decide consciously if those patterns are working for both of you. If it's not, then you can consider what would work better without getting caught up in only your own wants and desires. When you're living life effectively, it's like you've zoomed out to see the entire picture of what's going on instead of focusing on only one piece of the puzzle. Finding a more effective way to live life is the ultimate mindfulness experience.

KATE'S TIPS
Nonjudgmentally
I know that true mindfulness is a synthesis of all six "what" and "how" skills, but if I had to choose one of the six as most important, I would pick being nonjudgmental. It's also one of the most difficult to practice. Humans judge themselves and their environment almost constantly (the house isn't clean enough, I'm not working out enough, I shouldn't have eaten that, that driver is an asshole, this restaurant sucks, this item costs too much, etc.). It's a difficult thing to escape. But when you can let go of your judgments, even for a few minutes, it feels...amazing. So, how do you get there? Practice and patience. Before turning off your judgments, you need to notice them first. Spend a few days tuning in and noticing your judgments (especially the dreaded "shoulds"). Once you've gotten a handle on noticing them, see if you can work on shifting or changing them. So "the house isn't clean enough" might shift to "the house isn't quite how I'd like it, but it's not the end of the world." "I shouldn't have eaten that ice cream" could become "I'm working on eating less sugar, so I'll pay more attention to skipping ice cream tomorrow." Once you have some practice at shifting the judgments you make daily, you can start focusing on losing the judgments entirely for the moments you're practicing mindfulness. No more "the house isn't clean enough" or even "it's not where I'd like it." In mindful moments, you're striving for simply observing the mess or the things that are out of place, with no thought of how they "should" be any different than how they are now.

One-mindfully
Doing one thing at a time is really quite uncommon in modern culture. From engaging in multiple activities at once (texting while watching TV, for instance) to engaging in one activity physically while your mind is entirely elsewhere (such as planning out what you're going to buy at the grocery store while you're taking a shower), those moments when your body and mind are both engaged in the same,

singular activity are incredibly rare. So, it makes sense that it's difficult to achieve this state when practicing mindfulness. I find it easiest to start by trying to be mindful during tasks or activities that already fully (or nearly fully) engage me, such as cooking or working on a puzzle or painting. While being mindful of these activities, I get a sense of what it feels like to do something "one-mindfully," and I practice bringing my mind and my body back to the one task. From there, I expand to more mundane activities (like showering) because I've taken the time to really practice and get better at focusing. Like so many skills, it makes more sense to start in the shallow end of the pool, so to speak, as opposed to jumping in the deep end. When you are mindful of more rote activities, it can help you stay present when you do the task "out of order" (like washing the parts of your body in a different order than usual when showering).

Effectively

Everyone likes to be right; I'm fairly certain it's a part of the human condition. Some-times you might cling to the idea of being right so hard that it causes unintended negative consequences. Another thing you might cling to that gets in the way of being effective is wanting things to be fair. It's a perfectly normal human desire, but things aren't always fair, and you can't always be right. Sometimes trying to be right or make things fair actually makes your life harder or worse, or even prevents you from accomplishing your goals. Doing things effectively is really about letting go of your ego. Next time you approach a task with the intention of engaging with it mindfully, ask yourself if the way you usually do it is effective. If it's not effective, is it because you're clinging to the way it "should" work, or because you would rather be "right" than effective? If so, see if you can get out of your own way a little bit. Really lean into being objective and nonjudgmental, and see if you can identify and utilize an effective approach to the task at hand.

MICHELLE'S TIPS
Nonjudgmentally

Being nonjudgmental is about anxiety management for me. My anxiety is full of judgments, and while a small percentage of them may be based on facts, most are based on fear about something that is unlikely to happen. I catch myself regularly judging situations as safe or unsafe or "worth doing" vs. "not worth doing." When I walk into a new social situation, my brain starts making judgments about other people: who seems to be the most like me, the least like me, do I agree or disagree with the topics that are being discussed, etc. All of this can lead to me withdrawing and letting anxiety get the best of me because I start to close myself off to new and unfamiliar situations. This happens with a lot of things for me: new movies, new foods, new clothes, and so on. I'll make a quick judgment call of whether I like it or don't, and at times, this has truly prevented me from engaging in experiences that might be really great if I were more mindful in the moment. If you're like me, notice when your judgments are telling you something is "bad" or "unsafe" based on very little information. Take steps to try a new thing or talk to a person you don't know. You may be surprised how your world opens up when you decrease the number of judgments you have.

One-mindfully

The biggest tip I have to help you do things one-mindfully is to put your phone away. Most of us (myself, included) hardly ever do this. We tell ourselves we need our phones for one reason or another, and while that may legitimately be true at times, it's less true than we think. Doing something one-mindfully becomes difficult when your phone is receiving notifications and when it's easy to scroll through social media. Put it on silent, put it in another room, actually turn it off—whatever you need to do in order to fully give your attention to what you're doing in the moment. Of course, you don't have to put it away indefinitely; tell yourself you'll look at it again once you're done with the task at hand. Creating better boundaries in your life with your phone (and other electronic devices) helps you focus better and decrease distractions.

Effectively

Often, when you do something for the first time (or even the fifth or tenth time), you mess it up. You try one way to do it and it doesn't work. You try that way again and it still might not work. Eventually, your brain tells you to try something new and perhaps that works better (or it doesn't and you're back at square one). Regardless, you can be so afraid of trying something new because you've convinced yourself the way you're doing it is already working well enough. When it comes to living life in a more mindful, effective way, you are first required to take a chance and try something different. Only then can you discover new possibilities that may benefit you and explore uncharted territory. I encourage you to do something different in your day today: try to shower differently (like Kate suggests), season your food in a way you never have before, or take a different perspective in a conversation with someone than you typically would. If you want to take a deep dive into being more effective, ask someone you're close to about something you do that bothers them; their answer may surprise you. When you become curious about opening yourself up to change, you become less afraid of failure and more likely to stumble upon things that make your life better in ways you didn't expect.

PITFALLS

Pitfall 1

A common issue we hear from folks about being "nonjudgmental" is that they think it is dangerous or impossible. In the description of the skill, it even tells you to assess if something is safe or unsafe, *but to not judge it* (Linehan 2015). At first that may seem contradictory, but there is a real difference between assessing or evaluating something and judging it. Here are some examples of judgments: "I'm such an idiot," "She drives like she's drunk," and "He looks like a criminal." If we were to change those judgments into evaluations or assessments, they might look like: "I notice I make this mistake repeatedly," "She just swerved across four lanes," and "I notice I feel unsafe around him." In the judgments, there are sweeping assertions about the people. In the evaluations, there is noticing and reporting facts about the outside world or about thoughts or feelings. It could be unsafe or simply unfeasible to move through the world without making *any* evaluations or assessments about ourselves, others, or our environment, but it *is* possible to move through our world without making judgments, at least temporarily.

Pitfall 2

Some people say their brains or their lives make it difficult (or impossible) to do only one thing at a time. While doing only one thing at a time is the "gold standard" for practicing mindfulness, it isn't the only way to practice mindfulness. Think about being a new parent. When your child is young enough, it's nearly impossible to only do one thing at a time. You're almost always doing a task *and* thinking about or caring for your child simultaneously. Even when this is the case, you can still practice mindfulness! The intention of the one-mindfully skill is to be as fully present as possible. If "as possible" means you're still doing two or more things, then simply focus on being fully present to doing those two or more things. When you *can* do only one thing, then certainly do! But when your life doesn't afford it, simply do the best you can. That's all you can ask of yourself, and it is enough. Make mindfulness work for you. It's more flexible than you might think.

Pitfall 3

DBT uses the terms "effective" and "ineffective" a lot. In an effort to assess or evaluate their level of effectiveness, **people end up judging themselves if they did something that was an "ineffective" choice.** Just like we often say, "don't judge your judging," it's also important to not judge your effectiveness. If you start using it as a weapon against yourself, you're undermining a lot of what mindfulness is meant to do. Effective and ineffective are not synonyms for good and bad. When assessing if you're doing something in an effective manner, try to also remember the DBT tenet that we are all doing the best we can in every moment. If you've historically been ineffective when doing something, that's okay. Every time you approach a task, it's a chance to do it a little differently. Give yourself grace and cut yourself slack. We're all works in progress.

BENEFITS
Benefit 1
The reality is our judgments are often untrue. If we judge an experience before we've done it ourselves, we can't know how we would actually feel doing it. More often than not, our judgments reflect our "best guesses" about things. Sometimes those judgments lead to mistakes and miscommunications. While mistakes are inevitable in life, **if you adopt a nonjudgmental stance, you may find yourself making mistakes less often and considering alternative possibilities**. You may be more likely to ask questions and get curious instead of trusting your initial judgment of a person or situation. You'll be seeing things for what they actually are in the present instead of immediately assuming your judgments are correct.

Benefit 2
It has now been proven that the more things you try to do at once, the less productive you are (Rubinstein, Meyer and Evans 2001). If you're trying to talk on the phone, while checking your email, while also thinking about what to cook for dinner, while also listening to your child or partner talking to you...that phone call is not getting your full attention. **When we can actually do one thing at a time, our brain is less overwhelmed by all the other stimuli competing for our attention.** Mindfulness helps you learn and practice focusing on just one thing at a time, so you aren't exerting as much mental energy trying to do multiple things at once. The more balls you try to juggle, the more likely you are to drop one.

Benefit 3
When it comes to doing mindfulness effectively, it's important to focus on what reality is rather than what you want it to be. It's all too natural to think your way is the "best" way or the "only" way when that may not be true (and notice the judgment there!). You are effective when you can admit you're wrong and open yourself up to trying something new. Even if you don't like the way another person is doing the same task, **you can let go of your judgments and recognize that their way could be more effective than your way**. This can then lead to greater ease with doing the same task later that you never would have discovered if you had not been practicing mindfulness.

EXERCISE

Which of the "how" skills do you think will come most naturally to you, and why?

_____

_____

_____

_____

_____

_____

_____

Which of the "how" skills do you think you'll struggle with implementing, and why?

_____

_____

_____

_____

_____

_____

_____

What's one way you can start practicing the "how" skills in your daily life?

_____

_____

_____

_____

_____

_____

_____

_____

_____

PART 2

DISTRESS TOLERANCE

Distress tolerance skills help with navigating and surviving the hardships in life that you cannot change. Some examples of when to use distress tolerance skills include grief (either anticipatory grief or grief after a loss), relationships struggling or ending, and when you're refraining from problem behaviors.

Chapter 5

HALF-SMILE AND WILLING HANDS

ABOUT THESE SKILLS

Welcome to two of the simplest, yet most powerful, DBT skills out there. These skills are easy to do, don't require any mental work, and offer quick results. Let's talk about what each skill is, why they work, and when to do them:

- ○ **Half-smile:** A half-smile is a slight upturn of the corners of the lips without showing any teeth.

- ○ **Willing hands:** If you are standing with your arms by your side, turn your hands outward so your palms are open towards the same direction you are facing. You can also bend your arms at the elbow and turn your palms up to the ceiling. If you are sitting, turn your hands so that your palms face up to the ceiling, either with your hands in your lap or next to your thighs.

At this point, you may be wondering, "Is that it? There's nothing more to it?" Believe it or not, it really is that simple! You can either do each skill by itself or you can do both together for double the impact. Though you don't have to do either one for long, make an effort to do it for at least 60 seconds.

So, how does this work? Extensive research has been done about how our brains and bodies communicate with one another. In psychology, emphasis is often placed on how your thoughts impact your behavior (in other words, what goes on in the brain impacts the body). If you change your thoughts, the action that follows will change as well; this is referred to as "top-down processing." We now know our bodies can impact our brains, too. What you experience with your body directly changes your thoughts. This is called bottom-up processing (Rousay 2021). Similar to TIPP and self-soothing with the five senses (see Chapters 8 and 13), half-smile and willing hands are "bottom-up" skills: you do something with your body, and the neurons firing in your brain change as a result.

Half-smile works because smiling is associated with feelings of joy, peace, and contentment. Your brain learned over time that when you experience something positive, you smile. Studies show that even if you don't feel joy, the mere act of smiling signals to your brain to fire the neurons associated with happiness. Darwin was the first person to notice this and coined it the facial feedback hypothesis. This was proven in a study where participants held a pen horizontally in their mouths. Sure enough, they felt increased happiness after because their mouths had been forced into a smile shape while holding the pen (Strack, Martin and Stepper 1988).

Turning the palms upward with willing hands is common in many religions and is often done in yoga. Without realizing it, you make hand gestures with your palms turned up when communicating with others. Upturned palms signal vulnerability and openness to others, helping them to trust us and indicating you trust them (Pease 2014). Open body language also signals to your brain that you are safe, as it is a natural response to cross your arms for protection from a threat (Moore 2020). When you feel safe, your parasympathetic nervous system is activated, slowing your breathing and heart rate (Van Der Kolk 2014).

Half-smile and willing hands are distress tolerance skills because of their ability to bring a sense of calm, even momentarily, to a stressful situation. They can be done with other distress tolerance skills such as IMPROVE (to promote relaxation and to do one thing in the moment) and self-soothing with the five senses (such as doing a half-smile while inhaling a favorite scent or listening to music). Many people practice half-smile and willing hands as a mindfulness practice, intentionally doing either a half-smile or lying down with willing hands when they first wake up or just before bed. Half-smile and willing hands can also be used when practicing opposite action (see Chapter 17) to shift an emotional experience that doesn't fit the facts of a situation.

Both half-smile and willing hands can be done nearly anywhere for any reason, but there are some specific contexts where it may be helpful to use one instead of the other. Half-smiling helps more with depression or anger, while willing hands is more helpful for anxiety. Some people prefer to half-smile when they're alone and use willing hands when they are engaged in conversations with others because willing hands can be done with more subtlety. Because half-smile does not involve using your hands, it can be used when you're driving, doing housework, and so on, and this leads to some people using it more often than willing hands.

KATE'S TIPS
I'm a bit of a fangirl when it comes to half-smile and willing hands. I love the neuroscience behind the skills and how easy they are to do.

Half-smile
While half-smile is intended to be just a slight upturning of the corners of your mouth, holding that position can actually be really hard for my face! When I smile, I tend to smile big, with lots of teeth. Trying to hold a tiny smile on my face often

leads to discomfort and weird muscle twitches. For half-smile to really work for me, I use a bigger smile than recommended! I'm not suggesting you jump off the deep end straight into a maniacal grin, but feel free to modify the size of the smile a bit to better suit your face/comfort. The idea is to feel better, not to make your face hurt or make you self-conscious. Also, it's perfectly normal for your face to slip out of a half-smile if your mind wanders. Try to be compassionate towards yourself here, and just return to your smile when you realize it slipped away.

Willing hands

My suggestion here is to utilize willing hands just for yourself when you are alone, and not just in interpersonal situations. While willing hands is a wonderful skill for difficult, scary, or stressful conversations, it can also really help you calm down on your own. The same signals of safety are being given to your brain by assuming that position whether other people are around you or not. If I am having a panic attack, I will use willing hands (along with paced breathing) to help me return to equilibrium. If I am angry about something, sitting with willing hands often helps me find a sense of calm. There are a surprising number of circumstances in which willing hands can be of great use.

MICHELLE'S TIPS

I absolutely adore the versatility and ease of half-smile and willing hands. I regularly catch myself using the excuse of being "too busy" to use skills, but that doesn't work with half-smile and willing hands; like mindfulness, they can be done nearly anywhere when doing anything.

Half-smile

I use half-smile the most when I'm driving. Driving represents a transition as you move from one location to another. Driving also reminds you of how much is out of your hands: you can't control other drivers, whether you hit a green light or a red one, or how bad traffic is. As you sit in your car, traveling to your next destination, half-smiling can really help if you start to notice yourself feeling stressed. I often let my mind wander when driving, and it tends to wander to my to-do list and planning out my day. While this sometimes eases my mind to prepare for what's coming next, it can also lead to feeling overwhelmed. Since I can't use willing hands while driving, I half-smile for just a moment and I notice the effects almost instantly.

Willing hands

Whenever I tell myself I "don't have time" for something, that's exactly when I need to pause for just 30 seconds to breathe. Adding in willing hands helps in these moments and makes it more likely I'll breathe in a restorative way instead of taking shallow breaths. I think it's especially important to choose willing hands here over half-smiling (though you can certainly do that, too!) because willing hands forces you to stop what you're doing when you're busy. I also use willing hands when I'm watching TV, and it helps me stay more grounded and present as I watch without feeling tempted to look at my phone. It really is a mindfulness practice to use willing hands in this way more than it is distress tolerance. See how long you can do it for when you're engaged in an activity where your mind may wander.

PITFALLS
Pitfall 1
This first pitfall falls under the category of "your mileage may vary." While some people who practice half-smile and willing hands notice large-scale changes to their experience or mood from using the skills, they are the minority. For most folks, **the changes that come from using half-smile and willing hands are going to be more subtle.** Instead of going from depressed to joyous, you might go from sad to fine. While there is a noticeable and appreciable shift, it's not a wild swing. If you try this skill, work on being mindful while you practice it, so you are better able to notice smaller shifts in your experience. If it seems like the skills aren't working, ask yourself if you were perhaps expecting more from them than they could deliver.

Pitfall 2
Just like you may need to use some TIPP to bring your emotions down a bit before you can effectively self-soothe, you may need a more robust skill before half-smile and willing hands will be able to have an impact. **On a 1 to 10 scale of emotional intensity, if your current emotion is any higher than a 5 or 6, these may not be the correct skills to start with.** If you find that the skill seems to not be working, take a moment to ask yourself how intense your current emotions are. If they are on the intense side, try another skill before coming back to try half-smile or willing hands again.

Pitfall 3
It is absolutely normal to want instant gratification. When you're upset, you want that to change as fast as possible. It can be easy to flit from skill to skill, not giving any of them enough time to be effective. **Half-smile and willing hands in particular take a little while to fully work.** Your brain has to notice the changes in your body, notice that you are maintaining them, and then start shifting the chemicals around. While you may experience *an* amount of instantaneous relief, it's much more likely that you will need to use the skill for a minute (or five) before you experience the full benefit.

BENEFITS
Benefit 1
Half-smile and willing hands are two of the easiest DBT skills to remember. Compared to acronym skills where it can be difficult to recall what each letter stands for, half-smile and willing hands are simple skills to comprehend. **Not only is it easy to remember how to do each one, but it is also convenient and easy to build them into a daily routine if you choose to do so.** Intentionally half-smile while you're taking a shower or decide to use willing hands every time you talk with your partner at the end of your day. You can set random alarms on your phone reminding you to pause for a minute and do one or both. Half-smile and willing hands can be done for any reason at all, whenever you think of them. They can make any moment just a little bit better.

Benefit 2
While some DBT skills take time to do fully, **half-smile and willing hands are two of the quickest skills, taking only a minute or two to do.** One of the barriers that people commonly run into with DBT is not devoting enough time to a skill to see if it will truly "work"; they rush through it or try it for just a few minutes before declaring it a "failure" and moving on because it didn't provide the quick fix they were looking for. Though it is technically still possible to rush through a half-smile and willing hands, it's hard to argue with the quick turnaround most people notice when they do either one or both for just a couple of minutes. It's a bonus that they can also be done while engaged in other activities, so you don't even need to stop what you're doing to feel them working.

Benefit 3
Half-smile and willing hands can stand alone as skills to use, but as we've also discussed throughout this chapter, they can be woven into many other skills from different modules. In addition to using half-smile and willing hands as a mindfulness practice and when doing opposite action, you can use willing hands while using any interpersonal effectiveness skill to help regulate your nervous system and signal openness to the other person (even if they don't consciously notice you doing it!). Additionally, you can half-smile when you want to practice willingness instead of willfulness or when practicing cope ahead. Finding it hard to access your wise mind? Let half-smile and willing hands help you get there. **With nearly any DBT skill you can think of, adding on half-smile or willing hands to it creates a bigger impact.**

EXERCISE

When you try out half-smile and willing hands, does one of them seem to come more easily or have more of an impact? What do you notice when you practice each one?

Was there one of the two skills that you simply didn't like at all? If so, why not?

Between half-smile and willing hands, which can you see yourself using the most in your day-to-day life, and why?

Chapter 6

ACCEPTS

ABOUT THIS SKILL

ACCEPTS is all about distraction. At times in your life, you'll experience stressful or overwhelming situations that feel all-encompassing. Examples include a romantic relationship ending and you can't stop thinking about your ex-partner, worrying about an upcoming test even though you've studied hard, or coping with the death of a loved one. While it's completely natural to spend a considerable amount of mental energy focused on situations like these, you might find yourself needing a break every once in a while to focus on other things in your life or just to enjoy yourself for a little bit amongst the stress.

ACCEPTS offers you seven different ways to distract yourself. The two of us call this a "DBT buffet" skill—you get to pick whatever component you want to try. You don't have to do them in order, and you don't have to do all of them, the same way you don't have to sample every kind of food available at a buffet. It's also important to note that this is a time-limited skill. We do not recommend using distractions all day, as this can lead to emotional avoidance. Try one part of ACCEPTS for between 10 minutes to an hour and notice how you feel after.

ACTIVITIES

Find a task/project/hobby to do that's enjoyable and occupies your brain and/or your body. Activities can include any kind of physical movement (swimming, dancing, walking, etc.) or just about anything you might do around your house for leisure (reading, listening to music, playing a board game, etc.).

CONTRIBUTING

Contributing is all about finding a way to help someone else. The goal is to focus on another person's experience, which may help you feel less preoccupied by concerns in your own life. When we help others, we in turn feel better.

COMPARISONS

When practicing comparisons, you put a stressful/challenging situation you're experiencing into a larger context. You can compare a current struggle to a past struggle you've faced or compare a struggle you're experiencing to a struggle you see someone else experiencing, too. The goal is to feel less distress when you're reminded of how this current struggle compares to another struggle.

EMOTIONS

Choosing to intentionally create a new emotional experience can greatly reduce distress. This can be done by watching a funny movie or YouTube video or listening to music that's upbeat when you're feeling down (basically, taking in any kind of media or stimulus that influences your mood).

PUSHING AWAY

Tell yourself to not think about a painful situation for a set period of time. Use visualization to imagine yourself creating distance between you and the source of your stress, or use a mantra or phrase to push it out of your mind for a while.

THOUGHTS

Finding ways to occupy the mind can result in being so preoccupied with the mental task that you're no longer thinking about the stressful situation in your life. This can be done by counting objects in your house or out in public (e.g. counting things that are red), doing jigsaw puzzles or crossword puzzles, or playing games that take considerable mental effort.

SENSATIONS

When our bodies experience intense physical sensations, all our mental effort is likely to focus on our senses. Do something briefly that focuses on at least one of the five senses and feels intense. This can be done by taking a very hot or cold shower, eating spicy foods, or listening to loud music.

KATE'S TIPS
Activities

My favorite thing to do to practice activities is cross stitching. I do counted cross stitch, and it really engages my mind. If I get too distracted, I'll make a lot of mistakes, so I end up really focused. It's also nice because it uses my body to an extent, which helps it be more fully engrossing. I think the most important thing to keep in mind when choosing activities is that you want something where you're really engaged and unlikely to have your mind wander back to the distressing situation from which you're trying to take a break.

Contributing

This is one of my favorite components of ACCEPTS. The best example I have personally (which is certainly not available to everyone) is being a therapist. Sitting with and helping my clients always does an amazing job of giving me a break from my own struggles and distress. A more universally accessible way to practice contributing that I also enjoy is the simple act of holding doors for folks when I'm out and about. It's small and requires almost no effort, but it makes folks smile and helps me feel better simultaneously.

Comparisons

My favorite way to avoid the possible dangers of this component is to compare my *current* self to my *past* self. I still struggle with a variety of mental health issues. That being said, I struggle a whole lot less than I used to. I spent so much of my life filled with self-loathing and being suicidal, that however I'm feeling in the present is usually vastly better than how I felt for much of my life. I know that whatever I'm going through now, I've already survived worse. That gives me a sense of strength and confidence, knowing I will survive my current situation, too.

Emotions

Though it's rarely a mindful activity, watching TV is one of my go-to activities for emotions. I think it turns off just enough of my brain to dull the current emotions and pave the way for something new. I'll put on stand-up comedy, a favorite show, or a movie that usually results in me smiling or laughing. If you use TV for this skill, choose what you watch deliberately, not incidentally.

Pushing away

This one is a struggle for me! So many tactics for enacting this rely on visualization, something I'm incapable of due to having aphantasia. The technique I've come up with is to close my eyes, do some slow, deep breathing, and then say to myself, "Not now, later" over and over again. This is me telling myself now isn't a good time for the emotions coming up, and also promising myself I'll come back to them later.

Thoughts

This one is my favorite! I hear from so many clients that my favorite technique for employing this component has worked well and consistently for them. What I recommend is this: just start listing four-letter words that start with the letter "L." You can do this in your head, on paper, or on your phone (there are hundreds, so you're not going to run out). I love this technique because it's accessible and usually uses enough brain power to knock the distressing thoughts off their track.

Sensations

For this component, my go-to is listening to loud music. Either on a stereo or on headphones, cranking up my music creates an immersive experience for me, and often works to transport me away from the distress of the moment. It's especially helpful to me if it's music that makes me want to move my body/dance.

MICHELLE'S TIPS
Activities

Pick an activity that doesn't involve passively staring at a screen (this means watching TV or a movie or scrolling on your phone don't count for this one!). There's too much space for our brains to wander when we're sitting and not having to actively *do* something. Try to find a 15–30-minute block of time to devote to something you find enjoyable and see what happens. If it involves body movement, this will be even more distracting!

Contributing

My favorite way to contribute when I'm feeling stressed about something in my life is to think about someone I know who is also struggling or in need of some help. I text or call that person to ask how they're doing, or I offer to do something nice for them (e.g. watch their kids while they go run errands, go for a walk with them, etc.). Pick something that feels do-able for you and would be helpful for them; you'll both feel better.

Comparisons

You know the saying "misery loves company?" When I realize I'm not alone with big, hard situations in my life, I tend to feel better. While being in the "muck" of life sucks, it helps when I remind myself that other people have been there before me or are there with me currently. I try to not get in my head about "who has it worse" because every situation is unique. I just try to hear other people's stories if they want to share them and see which parts of their struggle resonate with me. I feel a lot less alone when I do this.

Emotions

Music is powerful when it comes to emotions. Thank goodness for playlists for different moods! Pick songs to listen to that will help you experience what you want to feel. If I'm having a day where I'm exhausted, I pick music that's likely to lift me up. If I'm feeling sad, I appreciate having one or two songs that will authentically bring a smile to my face.

Pushing away

Though I wish we lived in a world where we could always express what we're feeling without ramifications, I am well aware our world does not always allow for this, especially when it comes to workplace settings. I practice pushing away by telling myself when I will be able to express what I'm feeling, such as by saying, "I'll journal as soon as I get home" or "When I get to my car, I'll have a good cry." Having a plan makes it feel easier to be patient and focused on something else until that time comes.

Thoughts

There are so many ways to utilize thoughts that I love, such as doing crossword puzzles, wordsearch or sudoku. Lay out a jigsaw puzzle on a table in your house and challenge yourself to find five pieces when you need a little break. Working your brain is good for you and can be very distracting.

Sensations

I love taking a hot shower for sensations, but the key is to really focus on just the shower (see the following pitfalls section about mindlessness). Don't just take a shower like you typically would. Pay attention to how the water feels hitting your skin and how the soap smells. I also find it very grounding to put an ice pack on my neck if I'm feeling emotionally disconnected as a way to help me get back in touch with my body.

PITFALLS

Pitfall 1

One of the most common pitfalls of this skill is **the propensity for folks to engage in activities mindlessly instead of mindfully**. In the tips we wrote, you'll notice that many of the ways one can implement this skill are common, day-to-day activities. Many people might watch TV, read, do puzzles, listen to loud music, and so on, on a regular basis. Doing those things in the same incidental, mindless way you typically do them normally isn't going to get the results you're looking for with ACCEPTS. To get the most out of using this skill, remember to engage mindfully and with deliberate intent.

Pitfall 2

The intention behind comparisons is to gain a sense of gratitude, confidence, and possibly courage. **Used inappropriately, comparisons can lead instead to shame, embarrassment, and guilt.** Whether you're comparing yourself to another person or to a past version of yourself, the point is to use the comparison as a way to cheerlead yourself and boost your gratitude. If you find yourself thinking, "I've been through worse, so why am I struggling now?" or "Others have it so much worse than

I do, what right do I have to complain?," those are big, red flags. You can re-phrase those statements to say, "I've been through worse, so I know I have what it takes to make it through my current struggle" and "Others have it worse than I do, so even though things are hard, there are still things I am grateful for." Initially, the comparisons were used as a basis for being judgmental of the self. When they were re-phrased, comparisons were used as a foundation for increased self-confidence and gratitude. It's vital to use comparisons mindfully and intentionally, and in a way that is entirely self-compassionate.

Pitfall 3

The last pitfall is that of **trying all the things and then proclaiming the skill doesn't work**. In this pitfall, one might go from letter to letter through the acronym, not giving any one element the chance to *actually* work. This could look like watching a show for five minutes, then reciting five or six four-letter "L" words, then listening to loud music for a minute, and so on. If you decide to use ACCEPTS, give whatever component you choose the time to actually work. Each element and every person are going to be different, so the "right amount of time" can't really be nailed down. We recommend giving it *at least* ten minutes for one component, and maybe longer. If you're feeling rushed, you're probably not mindfully present. Do your best to find a mindful space, and give the skill a fair shot at working before you throw in the towel.

BENEFITS
Benefit 1

Distraction is like changing the channel in your brain. When your brain runs on repeat and seems to only focus on one thing it becomes draining, and your ability to focus on other tasks suffers. **Giving yourself a little break can make all the difference in feeling better able to balance all the things you do in life.** In a world where the to-do list seems to never end, taking a step back to distract yourself from the items on the list that may be stress-inducing allows you to then get them done more effectively. While it sounds counter-intuitive, you accomplish more when you pause periodically and take breaks (Rees et al. 2017). Those who are better able to catch overwhelm early and intervene are less likely to go down a rabbit hole of burnout. Intervening with distraction—especially intentional, time-limited distraction that uses your body to do something (such as with activities, contributing, and sensations) and changes your thinking (such as with comparisons, emotions, pushing away, and thoughts)—is powerful in helping you take care of yourself.

Benefit 2

Utilizing the different components of ACCEPTS can help shift your perspective about a current stressful situation. Participating in an activity you enjoy can result in feeling a sense of rejuvenation. Contributing can leave you with a "helper's high."

Comparisons can lead to a feeling of gratitude. Emotions can provide you with a quick jolt, injecting some immediate positivity into your day. Thoughts give your brain something else to occupy it. Sensations physiologically change your body. While none of these things can actually change the reality of a situation (if your boss is treating you terribly, these things won't result in your boss treating you well, for example), **they can provide you with a new experience that may help you feel better able to cope with the challenging situation you're currently facing**.

Benefit 3

Part of what makes ACCEPTS effective is how many components of it focus on connection with others. **When you contribute to someone or something you care about, you are reminded of your ability to make a positive impact, however small it may be.** If you're struggling with a life situation that has left you feeling hopeless, this can be a powerful remedy. Comparisons also help put challenges into perspective and can help you feel more connected with other people going through the same thing. Whenever you use emotions, you also rely on others: those who perform the songs you love or act in the movies that make you laugh. You have a different emotional experience because of something another person created. When you are able to connect with others during a difficult, isolating time in your life, your mood can greatly improve, and stress naturally decreases when you feel a sense of community.

EXERCISE

Of the seven components of ACCEPTS, which do you like the most, and why?

On the other hand, which component do you like the least, and why?

Can you imagine ACCEPTS being useful to you in your life? Where/how can you see yourself employing it the most?

Chapter 7

IMPROVE

ABOUT THIS SKILL

Similar to ACCEPTS, IMPROVE also has seven components and is a "DBT buffet" skill (pick as many or as few of these as you want to practice). Despite some definite similarities between ACCEPTS and IMPROVE, IMPROVE is used for an entirely different purpose than ACCEPTS. ACCEPTS is about distraction and giving you a temporary break from a stressful situation in your life. IMPROVE gives you skills to shift your perspective on your stressful situation and find a sense of peace or calm while you're experiencing it. A key distinction between ACCEPTS and IMPROVE is that overall, ACCEPTS is more action-oriented and focused on "doing." IMPROVE is more about "being," and many of the components can be done simply by shifting your thoughts and perspective while you're actively in a time of stress. You can typically see someone using the ACCEPTS skill; the IMPROVE skill is often more subtle and internal.

The unfortunate reality is that we can't always distract ourselves sufficiently when we are going through a time of tremendous stress, which means ACCEPTS is not always going to be the appropriate skill for coping with hard times. For example, imagine a parent who is in a hospital room with their child who is very ill. That parent may not want to distract themselves or find it difficult to do so; after all, they don't want to leave the hospital room, and they want to focus on being with their child as much as possible. Using IMPROVE could help this parent manage their own stress while being present at the same time.

IMAGERY

Bringing to mind an image that evokes serenity and joy can be a powerful tool for combating stress. You can think of an image of a calming place you've been to in real life or make up an image you find peaceful. If you are someone who can't visualize, you can think back on pleasant or enjoyable memories and how you felt then.

MEANING

Finding meaning in stressful times is going to be different for everyone. Some people find great comfort in thinking about how "everything happens for a reason," while some people hate that phrase. Oftentimes, we cannot find meaning when a difficult event is very recent or currently still happening, and that's completely understandable and okay. Finding meaning also doesn't mean understanding why the event happened in the first place; we may never truly understand why tragic things happen in this world. The reality is that stressful, hard things change you, no matter what. You are impacted by the things that happen in your life, both good and bad. If you become curious about the impact of a stressful event on your life, it's possible that that event (as terrible and awful as it was) may have shaped you in a way that had a positive impact on your life, however small. If you are able to find any kernel of good in a situation that was overwhelmingly bad, you've found some form of meaning.

PRAYER

Prayer is going to be highly individual. Some people pray by formally attending religious services and engaging in specific rituals to connect with a higher power. Others pray more informally when they are alone or find themselves wishing and asking for guidance or comfort from a higher power during times of great distress. While we are not here to endorse or recommend any specific religious practices, prayer can be one way to improve a difficult moment for many who do believe in some higher power.

RELAXING

While the word "relaxing" may invoke images of being pampered (e.g. going to a spa, having a bubble bath, etc.), there are many ways to relax that don't involve a lot of time, effort, or money. Take a few moments to stretch your body or breathe deeply. Drink a comforting beverage, like tea, or wear comfortable clothes. You can get more ideas on how to relax in the next chapter when we talk about the skill of self-soothing using the five senses.

ONE THING IN THE MOMENT

Remember when we talked about doing things one-mindfully? That's exactly what doing one thing in the moment is. When we "zoom out" on a big, stressful situation, we can easily feel overwhelmed by the enormity of how bad it is (or could be in the future). Doing one thing in the moment is "zooming in" on what's right in front of us. When you do this, you are intentionally choosing to focus on being present and only doing what needs to be done right then.

(BRIEF) VACATION

Unfortunately, having the "V" in IMPROVE stand for "vacation" does not usually mean taking a vacation. Most of us don't have the resources to take a vacation whenever we want to (especially when we're going through a hard time). Instead, "vacation" here means taking a break for a little bit. You can choose to take a break and use elements of ACCEPTS to distract yourself while you do so. A break (or brief vacation) can look like going for a walk around the block, taking a drive, spending some time with a friend, or making time to go to a place you enjoy close to home. It may last ten minutes, an hour, an entire day or multiple days, depending on what you are able to do. All forms of brief vacation have the benefit of changing your environment temporarily and giving you a reprieve from the stress you're going through.

ENCOURAGEMENT

Words are powerful and the words we tell ourselves (or hear from others) when we're going through a difficult time can have a lasting impact. Be mindful of your self-talk, and try to tell yourself things to lift you up instead of bring you down. Focus on what you're doing well, rather than what you could be doing better. Acknowledge the effort you're putting forth to cope and get through what you're dealing with. Need some examples? Check out our tips sections.

KATE'S TIPS
Imagery

This one I struggle with on a practical level, since I cannot picture things. To make this skill work for me, I use a couple of different tactics. The first is to externalize it. Instead of *imagining* a peaceful image, I *look* at peaceful/happy pictures (pictures online, pictures of my cats, or trips I've taken). The second is to simply reminisce about happy memories. Though I can't picture the memories, I can still "look back" in my imagination and experience some of the happiness and peace I felt at the time. If picturing things is difficult or impossible for you, you might try those tactics, too.

Meaning

I'm in the camp of people who don't like the phrase "everything happens for a reason." In fact, that phrase puts my proverbial hackles up immediately. In spite of that, I think meaning is my favorite component of IMPROVE. It can take me a while to see the meaning in terrible things (for instance, it took me a long time to see how the difficulties of my childhood helped to make me a better therapist), but finding meaning in past struggles helps me know I will likely find meaning in whatever I'm suffering through in the moment. Knowing that one day I'll look back and find the meaning helps me survive the moment. Try looking at things you like or admire about yourself now, and see if you can trace them back, even in part, to difficult events in your history.

Prayer

For a long time, I would have told you I didn't pray. I wasn't raised within any religious practice, and I didn't believe in any kind of higher power (which I thought was a prerequisite for prayer). Nowadays, I approach this differently. For one, there have certainly been moments in life where I thought simply, "Please help me." It was just a plea loosed to the universe at large, but I still see that as prayer. I am also inclined to see many mindfulness practices as prayer because they are moments of peace where you let go. Prayer for me is a peaceful or calm acknowledgment that I'm in a hard place and could use help and support. If you're like me and have felt like prayer wasn't for you due to being an atheist or something similar, consider that it may still be accessible for you, and play with ways you might achieve that state of calm.

Relaxing

How anyone likes to relax is going to be personal to them. For me, listening to music or reading books are the two most consistent and accessible ways I like to relax. Even brief doses (listening to just one song, reading for just five minutes) usually has a remarkably large effect on my mood. If something tends to easily impact your mood, see if there are ways you can utilize it in your difficult times, even just in small quantities.

One thing in the moment

There's a one-minute meditation I listen to frequently that has a line in it saying "... just for this moment, come back to harmony." I love this line, because it reminds me there's power in taking even just one moment to be at peace. I like just coming back to the moment and seeing if there's one thing I can do to improve or thoroughly enjoy what I'm doing—for example, taking a deep breath, savoring a sip of tea, tuning in to the feeling of the sun on my face, or adjusting my posture so my body is more comfortable. When my world is chaotic, overwhelming, or painful, sometimes all I can find is just one moment, so how can I make the most of it?

(Brief) Vacation

I have three words here: self-date day. Now, while brief vacation can certainly be accomplished in less time than a full day, self-date days are my favorite way to practice this skill. The basic tenet of a self-date day is that I only do things I want to do (no chores, no errands, no obligations of any sort). Sometimes this looks like taking a day trip to somewhere a couple hours away, and sometimes it looks like sitting around and reading a book all day. There are no rules stating that I have to leave the house or stay home. I try to get in a self-date day at least once a month. If you took a self-date day, what might it look like? Is that something you can give yourself?

Encouragement

Much like relaxation, what feels encouraging to one person may seem saccharine and false to another. The biggest tip I have here is to find what works for you. Try on different lines of encouragement to see what rings true. For me, the line "this too shall pass" is one of the most encouraging and reassuring things to tell myself. It also often works well to remind myself that I have survived worse. Other times, utilizing a dialectic like "there's a lot that really sucks right now, but I still have a lot to be grateful for" can help me pull through. Whatever works for you is the right thing, no matter what anyone else thinks of it.

MICHELLE'S TIPS

Imagery

While you can truly visualize *anything* that brings you a feeling of calm and relaxation, I can't help but think of nature images. I think about places I've been, so then I am thinking of a beautiful place I've experienced *and* a positive memory of how I felt when I was there. If nature affects you the same way, try to think of nature scenes first when you use this skill.

Meaning

I like the phrase "everything happens for a reason." Why? Because I can look back at my life and see how, if something hadn't happened (even though I hated that thing happening at the time), I wouldn't be where I am today. Most of the time it takes me years after the fact to understand and see any silver lining, but I remind myself of that phrase and in a small way, it makes enduring the hard things in my life a little easier.

Prayer

I grew up going to church and attending a small, Christian school. Prayer was very much a part of my daily life, but I didn't always like it, and it often felt like something I was supposed to do rather than something I wanted to do. As I've gotten older, I've found meditative practices that help me connect to the higher power I believe in. When I meditate and seek the wisdom of the universe, I feel at peace and cultivate a belief that I don't need to worry about things outside of my control.

Relaxing

I used to think relaxing meant doing as little as possible for as long as possible. I've now come to see that a little relaxation goes a long way. Instead of wanting to read a whole magazine in one sitting (an activity I find relaxing), I tell myself to read just one article before I switch to a different task and that helps me feel like I'm balancing work and play. I can feel the benefits I get from even just stopping for five minutes to do something I enjoy that's calming for me.

One thing in the moment

Mindfulness focuses on doing only one thing at a time so you can place all of your attention on a single task before you. Though this is similar, I think of "one thing in the moment" from IMPROVE as choosing to only think or worry about one thing at a time. Our minds often want to think ahead and plan for potential outcomes, but bringing it back to thinking about one thing in the moment greatly reduces worry for me.

(Brief) Vacation

I take brief vacations by going for walks or when I'm driving by appreciating the time to myself and listening to music. I sometimes also find it beneficial to just change the environment I'm in by doing small things like opening up the windows or working on my computer when I'm cosy in bed instead of at my desk.

Encouragement

Only tell yourself encouragements that feel authentic to you. You may hear all kinds of encouraging statements from other people that sound superficial, no matter how well intentioned they are. You don't have to tell yourself everything will be okay if that's too hard to believe. Some of my favorite personal encouragements are to tell myself "I am enough," "I am stronger than I think," and "I am loved and supported." These are all things I easily forget in times of stress. Telling yourself encouraging statements on a regular basis before a crisis hits can help you remember them when you're struggling in the future.

PITFALLS

Pitfall 1

While far from unique to this skill, one pitfall here is having unrealistic expectations. The kind of situations where you want to employ this skill are usually difficult and distressing. While we hope that IMPROVE can help to alleviate your suffering, it's not going to solve or end it. **If you go into a situation with your expectations set too high, then the skill is going to feel like it didn't help.** That, in turn, can result in you not trying the skill again. The best way to tackle this pitfall is to expect from the skill results it's capable of rendering. Whenever you try a component of the skill, try asking yourself a few questions. Do you feel *at all* better than before? If you don't feel better *after* the skill, did you feel any better *during* the skill? Do you feel at all more capable of facing the situation? Does the situation make sense to you now in a way that makes it feel more bearable? If you can answer yes to one or more of those questions, then the skill did its job.

Pitfall 2

Intimately linked to the first pitfall, this one centers on a sense of hopelessness. Not only is the situation you're in not in your control to solve or hasten to its conclusion, but even the skills we're suggesting won't *really* make it better. Given both those things, **it's easy enough to find yourself asking, "Why try? What's the point?"** For this pitfall, it's important to remember that everything is a matter of degree. The situation you're in may be truly awful, and it will still be awful after you practice the skill, but it may feel *less* awful. If you don't make the time to take care of yourself in some of these ways, it could make your awful situation even *worse*. Some things in life are too terrible to escape the horror of them, but that doesn't mean it's not worth it to do what you can to make a small, tiny reduction in the awful.

Pitfall 3

In many of the situations where you might find yourself wanting to utilize this skill, the **thoughts can arise that you are betraying someone or something by taking a break, or questioning how you can try to have fun or relax when you're facing a stressful situation.** Think of someone sitting at the hospital bed of a sick or injured loved one. When in situations like that, it is quite common to feel a sense of guilt about taking care of yourself. There are a couple of ways to address this. First, you are a better resource for others the more well-resourced you are yourself. If you can remain relatively or mostly functional, you'll be able to handle the situation better and be of more help to others. The other thing to remember is that your suffering isn't going to lessen the suffering of others. While there's some chance others may benefit from you taking care of yourself, no one wins from you neglecting yourself.

BENEFITS
Benefit 1

Most, if not all of us, are prone to worrying about things we can't control. We would love to have a crystal ball to predict the future and prepare for how things will turn out. Unfortunately, anxiety can build when you're trying to cope with a situation you can't change, such as a loved one's medical diagnosis, a death, or being laid off from a job unexpectedly. Instead of trying to control a stressful situation, **IMPROVE gives you the tools to let go and see the big picture.** For many people, turning to this skill helps them weather the storm of change and uncertainty. It can calm anxiety to be reminded that you can endure difficult times (and that you can do it with the help of a higher power, if this is something you believe in).

Benefit 2

During times of stress, transition and change, it's all too easy to focus on other people's needs instead of your own. This is a very common way people cope with stress. They may not consciously realize what they're doing until it occurs to them they haven't eaten all day and can't remember the last time they showered. **IMPROVE is a fantastic reminder to take care of yourself by taking mental breaks in small, manageable ways even if you're still attending to other people and things that need to get done.** The various components of IMPROVE can serve as replenishment when you start to feel like you're running on empty. Once you've "refilled your cup," you are then better able to cope with the stress you're experiencing.

Benefit 3

IMPROVE gives a framework for finding the silver lining during hard times. While it's important to not discount the pain and suffering that is inevitable in life (especially when a loss happens), **IMPROVE offers ideas for how to come out on the other side of that suffering once the initial devastation has passed.** For most people grieving a loss, they find themselves doing at least one part of IMPROVE to help them cope in the long term with the pain they experience (even if they have no idea they're using DBT!). Imagery helps you remember positive memories, meaning helps you find the lessons you've learned, prayer and encouragement help you find strength to keep going, relaxation and brief vacation help you take care of yourself, and one thing in the moment helps reduce worry.

EXERCISE

Which component of IMPROVE can you see yourself turning to the most,
and why?

Which element do you think you'll find the least useful, and why?

Where/how can you see yourself employing IMPROVE the most in your life?

Chapter 8

SELF-SOOTHING WITH THE FIVE SENSES

ABOUT THIS SKILL

Self-soothing with the five senses is one of our all-time favorite DBT skills. It's something people tend to not do enough of in their lives, and the bottom line is that it feels good to self-soothe. Parents soothe their children in various ways when they're young: backrubs, stuffed animals, and lullabies are just some examples. If you fast forward to adulthood, adults have a much harder time soothing themselves. Taking time to simply relax tends to fall to the bottom of long to-do lists, and it starts to feel like a luxury to take a bubble bath, curl up in a blanket with a warm cup of tea, or get a massage. The good news is self-soothing activities don't have to take much time and they pack a powerful punch for emotional healing, as you'll see in our tips sections.

Self-soothing is any activity that creates a feeling of peace, calm, ease, and relaxation using one or more of the five senses (sight, sound, taste, touch, and smell). Because each person has individual preferences for what they experience as relaxing, what is soothing for one person may not be for another. The most important part with any self-soothing activity is that it engages the senses strongly, resulting in a mindful experience. Remember when we talked about mindfulness as paying attention on purpose, in the present moment? That's exactly what you're doing when self-soothing. Whatever self-soothing activity you choose to do (whether it's for 30 seconds or 30 minutes), it will hopefully help press the pause button on experiencing stress, giving you a much-needed break. When you engage in soothing activities on a regular basis, your physiology calms because you are finding opportunities for rest (Chawla et al. 2020). This allows you to then feel rejuvenated as you move forward with your day after doing something calming.

Self-soothing with the five senses is a great skill to use for sadness or other tender emotions. While some skills, like TIPP, are designed to decrease "louder" emotions like anger or fear, self-soothing is meant to provide comfort and a feeling of safety. Oftentimes when we experience sadness and grief, this is exactly what we need. Sadness and grief can manifest physically and show up as sleep difficulties, appetite changes, fatigue, and lethargy. Turning to self-soothing during these times can help with weathering storms of mourning or depression. Self-soothing is also a great skill if you're wanting to practice being kinder to yourself. Any act of self-soothing is an act of self-kindness.

While it may be obvious that you have an array of options for how to practice self-soothing if you are at home, you may be wondering how you might practice this skill on the go. One way you can go about that is to make yourself a self-soothing kit. A self-soothing kit is just a small container stocked with your favorite small self-soothing items. You might throw in an essential oil, a hard candy, a tiny plushy, a picture you like, and a reminder for a song to listen to on your phone. The details will be personal to you.

KATE'S TIPS
Sight

These days, most of us have our phones attached to us at nearly all times, which is good news as far as this skill is concerned. Having a phone on you means you have access to pictures. Whether it's pictures you've taken yourself or just internet image searches of your favorite baby animal, phones offer a wide array of possibilities for use in self-soothing with sight. One other thing I really like is keeping something in your wallet. I once found this tiny card with a cartoon dinosaur holding a bunch of balloons in its mouth. Inside, I wrote "Cheer up!" to myself. I found it about 20 years ago, but it still brings a smile to my face every time I see it.

Sound

Music, music, music! For me, music is definitely what I seek out when I want to self-soothe using sound. Most specifically, I listen to lullabies (which I know may sound strange coming from an adult). I like to combine lullabies for sound with a nice soft blanket for touch, and just snuggle up and listen.

Taste

What are your comfort foods or beverages? For me, I think of creamy tomato soup, warm vanilla milk, tea, and top ramen (don't judge). If I have the ability to do so, I'll reach for one of these for self-soothing with the sense of taste. They are familiar, some are tied to fond memories, and they just help me relax. Unfortunately, none of those are very portable. If I'm setting up a self-soothing kit, I tend to go with small foods that have flavors I can luxuriate in or savor, like candies or chocolates. They're pleasant and intense enough that they help me focus on the moment and ground a little.

Touch

For me, there are two routes I take for soothing myself with touch. One can be summed up by the word "cosy": soft blankets, comfy pyjamas, fuzzy socks, things like that. The other way is through self-touch. This can be compassionate self-touch, like putting my hand over my heart, or this can be gentle and pleasant touch, like putting on lotion. While many aspects of self-soothing may be difficult to make portable, I find a lot of touch-oriented things can be easily taken with you. My two favorite things to put in a self-soothing kit for touch are lotion and fuzzy socks.

Smell

Smell may be my very favorite sense. It's the one I find the most soothing, and often the most uplifting. I am a person who very literally stops to smell the roses (and the lilacs, and the hyacinths, and the wisteria, too). When I'm at home, I really enjoy throwing fresh herbs, lemons, or mulling spices into a pot of water and just letting them gently simmer on the stove for hours. It fills the whole house with wonderful aromas, and that is often enough to brighten my mood. I also enjoy scented candles or wax melts. If I'm on the go, then I like using either a lotion that smells really nice (and works for touch, too!) or sometimes essential oils. What smells do you like? Are there ways you can make them portable too?

MICHELLE'S TIPS
Sight

Art is around us at all times, we just don't always notice it. Pause for just a moment, wherever you are, and find a piece of artwork to look at. You don't have to look at it for very long, but just see if there's something you can find about it that strikes you as beautiful or notice details that maybe you wouldn't spot otherwise. Art doesn't have to be a painting or drawing. Notice a wall color you like, or appreciate the shape of a staircase. You can also notice nature. Just as art is all around us, so is nature if we look for it. Notice flowers, grass, trees, or sand. Whatever you notice with your eyes, whether it's art or nature, I encourage you to take a deep breath while you're noticing. Even just looking for 10 or 15 seconds in a more intentional way with a deeper breath can be calming.

Sound

While Kate mentioned listening to music you find soothing, there is also benefit to noticing sounds we don't always pay attention to. Some people find the sound of rain or birds chirping soothing. If you're not able to hear nature sounds easily on a regular basis, consider buying a sound machine with nature sounds to put on in the background or search for videos online. Open up your windows if you can to let in these sounds, and start to pay closer attention to what sounds you like that are typically overlooked.

Taste

When you start to eat, take the first bite slowly and savor it. Most of us eat so quickly most of the time that we've stopped enjoying our food. It does not take a lot of time to eat just one bite slowly before eating at a normal pace and this can lead to noticing and appreciating your food more. It's also a good idea to have food on hand you find soothing, as Kate mentioned. Some of my favorites are chocolate, warm sourdough bread with butter, and macaroni and cheese. Many people like to chew gum or eat mints because they find it soothing, and it's easy to have those with you when you're out of the house as part of a self-soothing kit.

Touch

I love wearing comfortable, soft socks, sweatshirts, and infinity scarves. The clothes we wear touch our bodies all day, and there may be some textures you like and some you don't. Be intentional about your clothing choices, and wear clothes you truly feel comfortable in on days where you may need some extra self-soothing. I think it's also very important to have a stuffed animal to cuddle with; I don't care how old you are! Cuddling with a stuffed animal can be instantly calming. Petting or cuddling pets is also a great way to be soothed with touch.

Smell

I have a favorite lotion I put on every night before I go to sleep. It's quick and easy to do, and it really helps me fall asleep quickly because I like the smell of it. Using essential oils can also be powerful for regulating emotions. Choose smells you like or find calming; you can put a drop or two of the oil on your wrists or use it in a diffuser (make sure you follow the directions and guidance for the specific oil you choose). If you can, find smells from your past that you can bring into the present. You could do this by baking cookies or another favorite meal to bring good aromas into your home.

PITFALLS
Pitfall 1

Sometimes, people make the mistake of choosing the wrong kind of stimulus to employ for self-soothing, which can lead them to think it doesn't work. We have seen **folks assume that anything they enjoy counts as self-soothing, but this is not the case!** However much you may love a band's music, it may not be a good choice for self-soothing if it pumps you up instead of calming you down. Keep this principle in mind when choosing your self-soothing tools. Spicy foods, vigorous movement, intense music, icy cold or super hot showers...these things do not work well. When selecting the stimulus for your self-soothing, think about things that slow your heartbeat, make your muscles relax, and lead to you heaving a sigh of relief. Those are going to be the better things to choose.

Pitfall 2

A common issue we see people have with this skill is that they try to employ it in the wrong circumstances. While we love self-soothing, **it's not effective in all conditions**. If you think of unpleasant emotions as existing on a 1 to 10 scale, you really only want to employ self-soothing for emotions that are no higher than a 6 on that scale. For more intense emotions, skills like TIPP are more appropriate and effective. The only occasional exception to this is sadness or depression. Self-soothing can be an effective tool to use even with very intense sadness or depression. Though self-soothing won't fully resolve your sadness or depression, it may lighten it enough for you to engage in other skills or activities.

Pitfall 3

We have worked with folks who thought, "I'm supposed to choose things that relax me? Okay! Alcohol/pot/pills/etc. here I come!" We understand how someone might come to that conclusion, but it is dead wrong. **With this skill, you are trying to soothe or shift your emotions, not numb them out or escape from them.** While many intoxicants have some relaxing effects, they *all* alter your relationship with your emotions. Once the intoxicant wears off, you're right back where you started because you didn't process, soothe, or move through your emotions. If you want to sip a glass of wine in that candle-lit bubble bath you just ran yourself, we're not going to tell you not to. But if you reach for intoxicants first, or even include them to the point of *being intoxicated*, you're undermining the intent and efficacy of this skill. Self-soothing is best accomplished sober.

BENEFITS

Benefit 1

Self-soothe uses the body to calm the mind. There's very little thinking involved with self-soothing. For example, just tell yourself to hug a teddy bear and see what happens. When you're mindful of the activity and how it feels physically, you're likely going to notice your body starting to relax. When your body feels relaxed, this tells your brain you don't need to be worrying as much and that you are safe. **Self-soothing activities bring you into the present moment while providing a mental get-away from worrying at the same time.** You just have to do a physically calming activity for a few minutes and then see if your stress decreases ever so slightly.

Benefit 2

As we've already mentioned, using things to self-soothe that a child might turn to can still be effective in adulthood. Cuddle that favorite stuffed animal, make yourself a blanket fort, or eat that food your parents always made you when you were sick as a kid. These things not only provide soothing in the present, but also bring to mind happy or calming memories from childhood. If your childhood was full of trauma and you can't easily think of times where you felt soothed, this skill presents a beautiful opportunity for you to give yourself now what you needed then. **Treating yourself with kindness through self-soothing can do more than just relax you; it gives you simple things to do for yourself that rewire your nervous system and help calm you when you are emotionally triggered.** Remember what was said in the pitfalls: you don't want to use self-soothing when you're really flooded, but you can use it for mild anxiety or when you just need a reminder that you are safe.

Benefit 3

The reason why this skill is part of the distress tolerance module is because self-soothing activities can be really grounding when done mindfully, as intended. When big, difficult things happen in life, give yourself a break with something soothing. This can help you tangibly change your perspective. You can be experiencing something traumatic or stressful *and* you can also enjoy a cup of tea. It can be difficult to take pleasure in small things when you're in the midst of a crisis or experiencing significant depression. **Self-soothing can remind you to notice and enjoy the small pleasures in life, especially when you're trying to cope with something much larger.**

EXERCISE

Which of the five senses do you think will be the most soothing for you, and why?

What do you think might get in the way of you using self-soothing?

How can you imagine self-soothing being useful to you currently? Where/how can you see yourself employing it the most?

Chapter 9

PROS AND CONS

ABOUT THIS SKILL

The concept of "pros and cons" is well known and easily understood. When someone tells you to think of the pros and cons of something, they want you to consider the "good" and the "bad" parts about it. Using the pros and cons skill from DBT takes this idea one step further and uses dialectical thinking to help you make a decision about whether to do or not do something. Rarely is any decision you make "all good" or "all bad." DBT recognizes this and uses the pros and cons skill to get you thinking about the parts others may overlook and the parts you may not want to see. Even a decision that seems obviously "bad" for you has some kind of benefit or reason why you do it; otherwise, you wouldn't be doing it in the first place! On the other hand, there may be a clear "right" or "healthy" choice, but you may find there are drawbacks or challenges with doing it you hadn't considered. Let's talk more about how to use this skill step by step:

1. Find a piece of paper and a pen. Draw a large square. Divide that square equally into four smaller boxes to give yourself a 2 x 2 grid.

2. Label each box with the following headings:

    a. upper left box: Pros of doing this

    b. upper right box: Cons of doing this

    c. lower left box: Pros of not doing this

    d. lower right box: Cons of not doing this.

3. Start making a list in each box of everything you can think of for each category. Use extra paper or write in the margins if you run out of room.

DBT designed this skill to address "problem behaviors." A problem behavior is anything that interferes with your health and well-being; we all struggle with problem behaviors from time to time. Examples of problem behaviors include using drugs or alcohol, self-harming, staying up too late, watching a lot of TV, spending money excessively, and so on. For example, let's say the problem behavior you're struggling with is staying up too late at night and not getting enough sleep. Think about the pros of staying up late (i.e. what do you get out of this, what are the reasons for why you do it, how does it benefit you), the cons of staying up late (i.e. how does it negatively impact your life), the pros of not staying up late (i.e. what could be beneficial about going to bed at an earlier time), and the cons of not staying up late (i.e. what could make it challenging to do this, what would you be missing out on if this changed). This skill can be applied broadly, beyond just thinking about problem behaviors. Whenever you're facing a big decision in life, this skill helps you organize your thoughts about it in a new way. You can use pros and cons to decide whether or not you want to get a new job, move, stay in a relationship, or have a difficult conversation with someone.

After you've filled out your answers in each of the four boxes, you may wonder what happens next. Sometimes, the answer may come to you very clearly about what to do or not do. Other times, you may feel even more confused than before. This is not an uncommon experience, and it doesn't mean you've done the skill wrong. Some people find they are able to write a lot for some boxes and not for others. Other people find they did not write much in one of the categories, but that what they did write carries a lot of weight. We talk about this more in our tips sections to show how we use pros and cons personally and ways that may help you decide what to do next for yourself after you've written in your responses.

KATE'S TIPS

I know this may seem strange to say, but this skill helped me feel seen when I went through DBT as a teenager. So much of how self-harm is reacted to is based on people thinking it has no benefit (that it is crazy, stupid, nonsensical, and more). Then along came pros and cons, and it actually had a space for me to list the *pros* of self-harm. When I was given an opportunity to name the pros to doing it, it helped me feel more seen and less judged than ever before. One of the reasons I still like pros and cons so much is because it can be used for so much more than self-harm and other so-called problem behaviors. I see it as a more complete, comprehensive, and thorough way to examine almost any big choice you might be facing.

Tip 1: Get real with yourself

Honesty is key to using this skill. If you aren't being honest with yourself while doing your pros and cons grid, you aren't going to get very helpful results. It can be very difficult, sometimes even embarrassing, to admit to the pros of some behaviors. But if you aren't being honest, it's almost a way of shaming yourself further. If you're engaging in this problem behavior without any reason, isn't that worse? It is also tempting to neglect the downsides of things you really want to do, but you're giving yourself short shrift if you do. Give yourself the respect you deserve, look honestly and openly at each category, and fill them in as thoroughly as possible.

Tip 2: Think long-term

The notion of being scrupulously honest with yourself extends past filling out the grid. Once you have thoroughly explored each option, you then need to be honest about which choice is best/healthiest. Just as it can be easy to downplay the cons of something you really want to do when filling out the grid, the same temptation exists when you look at the grid and try to decide what to do now. Make sure you are looking at and fully appreciating the consequences of those cons. If I were filling out pros and cons for self-harm, one thing that would go in the "cons of doing this" box would be that it could cause scars. Now, if I'm in a headspace where I'm really wanting to self-harm, it can be tempting to think things like, "I already have so many scars, does it really matter if I make a few more?" It would be really important for me to think about how I think/feel about my scars when I'm *not* in that headspace. I'd need to remember that my scars already cause me discomfort at times, especially in certain social situations. In other words, I would need to be honest with myself and look past the feelings, desires, or ways of thinking I'm experiencing at that moment.

Tip 3: Find wise mind first

Make sure you're accessing your wise mind while practicing pros and cons. Your pros and cons are likely to be skewed and far less useful if you approach the skill from only your reason mind or only your emotion mind. You need to bring both to the table in order to get a clear/full picture of the situation at hand. If you end up doing a quick pros and cons on the fly some time, and you know you were mostly in one mind or the other, it's a good idea to come back to that pros and cons later. Then you can flesh it out from more of a wise-mind perspective.

MICHELLE'S TIPS

In order to practice pros and cons the way DBT intended, it is recommended to create the grid as we described and write in your answers. While this can be helpful, it is only the first step in practicing pros and cons. People often feel limited if they don't have the means to write down their responses when they're facing an urge. There are many ways you can adjust this skill so you reap the benefits of doing it without facing too many roadblocks.

Tip 1: Look back at your pros and cons grid

One of the major pitfalls with this skill is that after someone completes their grid, they think they are finished with the skill. Pros and cons will only work in helping you make a change if you remind yourself of it regularly. I encourage people to put their pros and cons grid up somewhere in their house where they can see it every day or to take a picture of it and put it in their phone. This is really important if you're trying to overcome an addiction or any other behavior you do on a daily basis.

It can help to read your pros and cons answers every day and consider adding on to it if more thoughts arise for any of the grid quadrants. Revisiting it often is how you actually start to make a change.

Tip 2: Think about the questions in your head

Though there are benefits to writing things down, pros and cons can be done by thinking about each of the four questions and making a mental note of your responses. If there is one answer that stands out to you, focus on that and explore it further. That may give you some much-needed insight into why you're making this choice and how it's impacting you.

Tip 3: Think through different scenarios when making a decision

Another way to take this skill further is to play out different scenarios in your mind. What happens if you don't do this? What happens if you do? Let your mind explore what could happen in the immediate future or the long-term future. Though you don't have a crystal ball to predict anything with certainty, past experience provides valuable insight into what could happen again. Doing this also gives you an opportunity to think about if doing (or not doing) this action will result in you getting closer to or further from your long-term goals and the things you really want. Recognizing how this decision aligns (or doesn't) with the big picture of your life can be powerful in helping you choose what to do.

PITFALLS

Pitfall 1

So many people make a pros and cons grid and then put it somewhere where they never look at it again. If you do your pros and cons for something you encounter regularly (as opposed to for a one-time decision), you will get a lot more out of it if you see it often. Along with doing it and putting it away, another similar pitfall is to **only do the grid once, and then never revisit it**. If you have a behavior that is a consistent challenge for you, then we strongly recommend updating your grid every so often. Maybe that means once a year, once every month, or once every five years. You're going to know best how often this would be a good idea. You just want to make sure your pros and cons are current to the person you are *now*. Keeping it up to date helps to keep it relevant.

Pitfall 2

We often see people blame the skill or blame themselves if they wind up engaging in a problem behavior after doing pros and cons. **They might think that doing the skill in the first place was pointless.** They may think, "It didn't stop me from doing the problem behavior, so what good could it be?" This would be conflating their own difficulty with impulse control with the efficacy of the skill. Just because they engaged in the problem behavior after doing pros and cons doesn't mean that the skill is useless. They could also use the skill as a way of shaming themselves, too. They may think, "After all, I had it all spelled out, exactly why doing this was a bad idea. I had the consequences right there and did it anyway." Humans make decisions they know aren't the best choice nearly every day. No need to use this skill as a way of beating yourself up. This is a tool to help you support yourself in making better choices; it's not a magic spell that will keep you from engaging in your problem behaviors.

Pitfall 3

The final pitfall is what sometimes happens when the "right" answer goes wrong. It's important to remember that you cannot know the future. **Any time you're trying to think of the consequences of something, you're just giving it your best guess.** Because of this, sometimes you're going to get it wrong. You might sit down and do a thorough, wise-mind-led, honest pros and cons, and then enact the "right" choice...only to have it go horribly awry. If/when that happens, it can be easy to think the skill itself didn't work. While that could be true, it's more likely that you were simply mistaken in your guesses, which is a quintessentially human thing to experience. The skill was still a good idea, and it helped you come to the best decision you could with the information you had. You just couldn't know the future.

BENEFITS
Benefit 1

Pros and cons increases self-awareness. So many decisions are made rapidly (within milliseconds!), and we don't take time to pause and consider why we do the things we do (Paddock 2017). **Pros and cons offers a chance to pause and look deeper.** As Kate mentioned in her tips section, the more honest and transparent you are about the pros of doing the behavior, the more understanding you'll get. The first step to any kind of change is to understand the rationale behind *why* you are doing what you're doing. Once you know this, you can make a new choice to help you get that same need met in a new, healthier way. If you don't know why you're doing what you're doing, you'll be more likely to go back to the same familiar way you've done things before.

Benefit 2

Pros and cons remind you that you have control over choices you make. In nearly every situation, you have a choice to either do or not do something. Even if you rationally know this, it's hard to remember in the moment when the pull to do a problem behavior is overwhelmingly strong. **Pros and cons shows what barriers may be in the way of doing a healthier action.** This leads to further thinking about how to overcome these barriers once you are aware of them. When you pair this with the increased self-awareness that comes with doing this skill, you will hopefully start making more intentional decisions in your life.

Benefit 3

A commonly asked question is, "Why do you do that if you know it's not good for you?" Pros and cons can provide the answers. Others in your life may judge and disapprove of the decisions you make; don't use their viewpoints to cause further shame and embarrassment about the choices you've made up until this point. **Sharing with others what you think about when doing pros and cons may help them better understand your decision-making.** Even if they struggle to support you in the way you would like, sharing your pros and cons can be a positive step towards helping you communicate your thought process to others if you choose.

EXERCISE

What do you find you like or dislike about the way DBT does pros and cons?

What's one behavior of yours you could do pros and cons for?

Where do you think this skill will prove to be the most useful to you currently, and why?

Chapter 10

RADICAL ACCEPTANCE

ABOUT THIS SKILL

In our opinion, radical acceptance is the hardest DBT skill to do. It also has the power to be one of the most life-changing skills when you are able to practice it. It is a skill to use when you are facing the most difficult things in life, the things you cannot change and that are likely causing you a significant amount of stress. Radical acceptance is the skill to use when you may be facing an injury or illness with no clear cause or treatment. It is the skill to use when your life circumstances may be drastically changing without your control or consent such as having to move suddenly or getting laid off from a job. Though radical acceptance is not an interpersonal effectiveness skill, you must radically accept things on a regular basis when it comes to a partner, child(ren), co-workers, and others. They may do things you dislike and won't change or stop doing those things, despite your best efforts to communicate with them. Life inevitably will present you with challenging situations that cannot be easily altered by you alone and, when these things happen, radical acceptance is the best, most powerful skill to turn to.

Different from many other DBT skills, there is no acronym here for different ways to practice radical acceptance. Understanding radical acceptance and then truly implementing it are different things; it's hard enough to do the first, and even harder to do the second. We hope our personal stories will help you understand how we recommend practicing radical acceptance, but for now, it's important to address what radical acceptance is. According to Linehan (2015), radical acceptance is "when you stop fighting reality, stop throwing tantrums because reality is not the way you want it, and let go of bitterness (p.342)." Let's break this down further.

WHEN YOU STOP FIGHTING REALITY...

Most of us, without truly realizing it, fight reality all the time. We want things to be as we want them to be rather than how they actually are. We want to believe that people in our lives will do what we've asked them to do. We want to believe that things will get better when we're experiencing hardship, and that a solution is just around the corner. And we want to believe that if we continue to act as though a thing isn't really happening that will mean it isn't happening. While this all sounds great on paper, what this does is stop you from working with what is and being mindful. It's common to think ahead to the desired future so you can ignore how bad the present is.

STOP THROWING TANTRUMS BECAUSE REALITY IS NOT THE WAY YOU WANT IT...

You never grow out of throwing tantrums, no matter how old you are. The tantrum might look different as you age, but it's very common throughout the lifespan to protest and have strong responses to things you don't like. Tantrums can look like refusing to engage in responsibilities, yelling/swearing at others or out of frustration with yourself, and doing what you want to do, even though it's not effective and could make a situation worse. Tantrums are all about control, so when you are facing a big life event that's overwhelming, throwing a tantrum is really an effort to express how much you don't like it and to try to control your environment.

AND LET GO OF BITTERNESS

When something big, unexpected, and awful happens in your life, you are not going to embrace it or be happy about it. Nobody is happy when they're told they have cancer or are served with divorce papers when they wanted to make their marriage work. Nobody likes it when their child is having challenging behaviors in school or when a boss is critical of their work. Because we don't like these things and wish they weren't happening, we can harbor feelings of anger that turn into resentment and bitterness. You might be going through the motions of what you need to do, acting like everything is fine, but internally you are hating what you're going through. While this is completely natural, feeling bitter doesn't serve you. It keeps you stuck in wishing reality was different than what it is. There is a middle ground here between hating something and liking it, and that middle ground is accepting it.

So if you're not fighting reality, not throwing tantrums, and not feeling bitter, then what are you doing instead? First, it's important to practice mindfulness and make efforts to be in a wise-mind state. As a reminder, wise mind is a place where you acknowledge and feel your emotions while also acknowledging the facts and logic of a situation. Radical acceptance requires that you use your reason mind to know what is in the here and now and your emotion mind to allow in your feelings about what's happening. Both of these components help you refrain from fighting reality and help you live more fully in it.

Second, you make efforts to determine within yourself and then communicate to other people what you feel and what you need. Because tantrums reflect an unmet need, you have to introspect to know what that need is. Unfortunately, you can't always get that need met, but you can at least know what it is, figure out why it might be there, and see if you can seek support from other people in the midst of the uncertain situation you're facing. All of that reduces the likelihood of tantrums erupting.

Finally, you can explore what other emotions you're feeling. There may be feelings of sadness, shame, or fear underneath the feelings of anger and bitterness. When you can allow yourself to feel those emotions—and even better, express them through tears, talking with others, journaling, or other creative outlets—you are able to decide what to do while you're feeling them. You're able to have greater compassion and understanding for yourself and experience more clarity about what decisions to make. This is much harder to do when you're unaware of what you're experiencing emotionally.

Unfortunately, finding your wise mind, knowing and communicating your needs, and being aware of underlying emotions is no easy feat. Many people, without even knowing it, seek out therapy because they are struggling to come to terms with a difficult situation in their lives they feel powerless to change. It's not enough to just see a situation for what it is and to look at the facts of the matter. *Radically* accepting something is different than simply accepting it. Accepting something radically means to look at all aspects of it, even the most painful parts, and to then determine your next steps. This often looks like a big shift happening that you would not have wanted to do otherwise, but you recognize what you need when you see reality for what it is. When you accept that change or transition is happening, you are better able to roll with the change than resist it and wish it was not happening in the first place. This is the goal of radical acceptance.

We have found over years of leading groups that the best way to explain radical acceptance is through sharing personal examples from our own lives. In every other chapter of this book we share tips, but radical acceptance is different. For this skill only, we share our stories instead. We hope you will find insight and helpful guidance woven into our experiences as you continue reading.

KATE'S STORY

Over the course of my life, there have been countless situations in which I could have made good use of radical acceptance. Some of them I accepted (even before I had been taught radical acceptance as a skill), and some of them I struggled against to the bitter end. There's one story I usually tell when teaching this skill and I will share it here. Hopefully hearing it will help you better see what radical acceptance is, some of the benefits of it, and how it can be a lifelong road to travel.

I always knew I wanted to have children. I actually have a memory of the moment I realized I wanted to be a mom. I was taking swimming lessons at the YMCA when I was around three or four, and there was a mom giving her infant a bottle. The mom allowed me to hold the bottle for the baby for a minute, and I was sold. My conviction never wavered from that moment on about wanting to become a mom myself. This made it especially heart-wrenching when, at age 17, I got pregnant and chose to terminate the pregnancy. It was absolutely the correct choice at the time, but my greatest fear was that it was my only chance in life to be pregnant and have a child.

Fast forward to my early 30s. I elected to get off hormonal birth control entirely, and instead switched to the copper IUD. Relatively soon after getting off hormonal birth control, my period stopped. I wasn't pregnant, but I wasn't getting my period either. This is about the point in the story where I stuck my head firmly in the sand and didn't come out for months (about four months, to be exact). After four solid months of no period, I finally went to the doctor. He blew me off, calling what was happening "irregular periods." A few more months went by, still with no period, and I was able to get in with an obstetric gynecologist (OB-GYN). I ought to mention that during this time I was fighting apparent reality *hard*. I did not want to even consider the possibilities of what all this meant. I dismissed, stomped on, and stuffed my ever-growing sense that something was *wrong*. Despite my intuition telling me I was going into premature menopause, I was studiously ignoring it.

But then, my fears and intuitions were proven right. After the visit to the OB-GYN, I learned that I was, in fact, in early menopause. After much testing at a fertility clinic, I was told I have idiopathic premature ovarian failure. In layman's terms, my ovaries were no longer responding to the hormonal signals my body was sending them, but no one could figure out *why*. To put it even more simply (and bluntly), I was sterile. Despite having it spelled out to me in no uncertain terms, I still "fought" with reality for a while. The doctor had mentioned that with the correct hormonal treatments, I *might* have a 4 percent *cumulative* lifetime chance of getting pregnant. I clung to that for all it was worth, for a while. But slowly, inch by inch, I started to let go. When I finally really started the process of radical acceptance, I landed in an ocean of grief, the likes of which I had never experienced. My whole life I'd *known* that I was going to be a mom. The notion that I would eventually be a mother was absolutely core to my sense of self. Having that ripped away left me feeling...profoundly lost and cut adrift. On top of having my entire sense of my future taken away, I was now also living in a world where my worst fear had come true. I'd always been terrified that the pregnancy I terminated at 17 was my only chance...and it had been. I'd terminated the only pregnancy I would ever have. To say my heart was broken would be an understatement of monumental proportions.

This is where radical acceptance really comes into play in my story. I had to accept, and accept, and accept again the facts: that I was never going to carry a child that was biologically mine, that my insurance didn't cover in-vitro fertilization—and I sure as shit couldn't afford it myself—and that adoption was as expensive (or more) and therefore also out of my reach. I had to accept it every time I saw one of the children's books I had collected. Every time I saw other women with children. Every time I had to buy the hormone replacement therapy I needed in order to not get osteoporosis in my 30s. So many things were reminders of the reality I didn't want to, but had to, learn to accept. In fact, there are still reminders. There are still days that I really struggle to accept it and I imagine there will always be days where I struggle. Radical acceptance can definitely be a lifetime journey, but I've found it worth it. It may have been "easier" to deny reality, but I never found even a modicum of peace until I found acceptance.

MICHELLE'S STORY

I am stubborn. I am the type of person who is used to pushing through discomfort and overcoming any obstacles in my way so I can achieve my goals. Most of the time, I persist enough to be successful. Other times, life has different plans. There was a major turning point in my life where I became painfully aware that no matter how hard I tried, life was not going to go according to my plan. I had to radically accept what was happening to find a new route forward.

From the age of four, I was a ballet dancer. I began dance classes once a week where we practiced jumping over teddy bears and dancing with scarves. Eventually, this turned into dancing at one of the top ballet schools in the country six days a week. Dance was my passion, and I wanted to perform in a professional ballet company after graduating from high school. I had no back-up plan for my life; for me, dancing was the only future I envisioned for myself. I was thrown a huge curveball when I injured my hip at 16. My injury happened gradually over time, and no one in my life knew that anything was different at first. I ignored the pain for a long time, doing my best to dance as if nothing was wrong. I didn't want to tell anybody because I didn't want to have to stop dancing. Eventually, I was limping as I walked, and I couldn't hide it anymore. I did physical therapy for months until it was clear that it wasn't working. It was determined that I had torn the cartilage around my hip socket and would need surgery. After surgery, I wanted to recover and return to dancing; I still had hope that I could get back to dancing how I used to. A year later, I needed a second, more intensive surgery, and that was the moment I finally radically accepted that I would not be able to dance professionally. I was forced to look at what else I could do for a career, and I decided to become a mental health counselor.

With radical acceptance, I often think about the expression "better the devil you know than the devil you don't." This is what keeps us in situations that don't serve us; we know the situation isn't good, but we worry making a change will be worse. I didn't want to stop dancing because I didn't know what else I would do, and I didn't think I could love anything as much as I loved dance. It takes time to see that things are truly not getting better and for us to eventually let go. Give yourself all the time you need before you feel ready to make a change. I needed *years* before I was ready.

Radical acceptance is like a maze. You're likely going to hit many "dead ends" before you find your way out and decide what needs to change. This is why I danced for months in pain because I kept thinking my hip would heal on its own. I tried physical therapy, wearing shoes with special inserts, medication and more before it was determined that surgery was the only option for me. You may be going through a similar process with a stressful situation in your life and find yourself exploring many different paths, trying to find a way through. Eventually, you may grow weary of this because it is emotionally and mentally *exhausting*. Others may tell you to stop this process long before you feel ready to. Though they may be right, listen to your own voice and inner knowing above all else. Only you will know when it's time to let go, and if you're not ready yet, then don't.

It's also crucial to know what you're going to do next when you radically accept your circumstances. I felt more at peace about no longer dancing once I decided I wanted to study psychology in college. Sometimes, we want things to stay the same because we don't want to think about the logistics of change. We don't want to think about what happens next if things don't go according to plan. I remember thinking to myself, "What do I do if I'm not dancing?" Ask yourself the scary questions and come up with an answer. I thought, "Well, then I'll go to college and try to find something else." I found my answers when I looked at the thing I was afraid to face. It's absolutely terrifying, and you're also strong enough to do it. I believe in you.

PITFALLS
Pitfall 1
The most common mistake people make when they think about or try to practice radical acceptance is thinking that it equals approval. Folks will fight hard against the notion of radically accepting their situation because they hate it. **They think that radical acceptance will mean they have to like it or think it's fine.** This could not be further from the truth. To use Kate's story as an example: she still, to this day, abhors the fact that she is sterile. It's a pain and a loss from which she may never fully recover. She doesn't approve of the facts of her story *at all*, but she accepts the facts. Because the facts just *are*. Whether she accepts them or not has no bearing on whether they *are*. We would never ask you to approve of a bad or difficult situation. We do not want you to lay down and passively accept whatever shit life slings at you. But we do suggest simply coming to terms with reality so you can spend less of your energy fighting against acceptance, and turn your energy towards taking action (where possible).

Pitfall 2
Along with thinking that radical acceptance means approving of the situation, **there are many people who think that accepting a situation for what it is means letting go of trying to change it.** Nothing could be further from the truth! Radical acceptance is actually one of the best and sometimes most important tools of change. How can you change a thing if you haven't accepted it for what it is? As a silly example, it is awfully difficult to problem solve how to get out of a locked room if you deny you're even in the room to begin with. You have to see the situation

you're in clearly, without blinders, before you can take meaningful action towards change. Practice radical acceptance first, and then take action. Going back to Kate's story, she would never have looked into how to go about doing IVF, or adoption, or fostering kids or anything like that if she hadn't first radically accepted being sterile. While most of those options aren't within reach for her at this time, she would never have known that if she hadn't looked.

Pitfall 3

Many of the skills in DBT are meant to help you feel some degree of better the moment you go about practicing the skill. That is not the case with radical acceptance. **In fact, quite often you feel mildly to substantially *worse* immediately after starting to practice radical acceptance.** After all, you've probably been denying reality because it is uncomfortable or painful in some way. Once you stop resisting, that pain and discomfort are going to come home to roost. But that's okay. Once that pain shows up, you have the opportunity to deploy other skills as needed to take care of yourself emotionally (or not). Some pain is good, and healing, and appropriate to feel. Either way, don't think that radical acceptance is not working because you feel worse after doing it as opposed to better. Instead, the sudden worsening of your emotional experience is more likely to be a sign you're doing the skill correctly, and it's working.

BENEFITS

Benefit 1

There is a difference between pain and suffering, and radical acceptance reduces suffering. A teaching from Buddhism says, "Pain is inevitable, but suffering is optional." Whenever we face painful events in life, we have a choice with what happens next. We likely feel a very strong emotion about the event, such as sadness or fear, and then we decide what to do with that emotion. For many people, they try to escape or avoid the thing causing them pain. Both of us mention doing this in the stories we shared about our own journeys with radical acceptance. Unfortunately, that only led to suffering and a worsening of our pain. **The sooner you can radically accept the painful things in life, the more likely you are to suffer less.** To be clear, this doesn't mean that the pain goes away once you accept it. The painful thing still exists, but you can ask yourself, "Now what?" after you've accepted it.

Benefit 2

Linehan (2015) says, "Acceptance may lead to sadness, but deep calmness usually follows" (p.342). There are many things in life we do not want to accept because we dislike them and wish they weren't happening in the first place. We feel sad that these things are happening. Kate felt sad about learning she wouldn't be able to have biological children. Michelle felt sad when she learned she had to give up on her dreams of dancing professionally. But once you know the outcome of something, when you really see it clearly for what it is, your brain does not need to work so hard to help you make sense of it because you know what it is. Not having answers is sometimes worse than having them, even if the answer you get is a painful answer. For example, though Kate dislikes not being able to have biological children, she felt more calm after being told she can't than when she was still searching for answers from doctors who were giving her inaccurate information. Michelle felt sad about no longer being able to dance, but felt calmness follow when she decided to turn her attention to figuring out what else she could do for a career. **Once you radically accept something, oftentimes the anxiety or worry you were feeling about it lessens.**

Benefit 3

When you radically accept something, there is potential for your life to change for the better. This may come years later and is not a guarantee that something better is in store for you after a devastating event occurs. Dialectical thinking is key here because an event can be life changing in both bad and good ways. Linehan (2015) says, "The path out of hell is through misery. By refusing to accept the misery that is part of climbing out of hell, you fall back into hell" (p.342). Accepting things fully is the first step to making decisions that may potentially change the direction of your life and free you from "hell."

EXERCISE

Reading about radical acceptance, is your immediate response positive or negative? Why?

Can you think of a time you've already used radical acceptance in your life? Describe it briefly here.

Can you imagine radical acceptance being useful to you in your current life? Where/how can you see yourself employing it?

Chapter 11

WILLINGNESS VS. WILLFULNESS

ABOUT THIS SKILL

Most days, you probably experience events you dislike. There's too much traffic on your commute. Your partner didn't do the dishes (again). You wanted to go for a walk, but now it's raining. Life does not always go according to plan; in fact, it rarely does. When things are not going as you hope, you have two options before you: to be willful or to be willing.

According to Linehan (2015), willfulness is "insisting on being in control" and "refusing to make changes that are needed" (p.346). More or less, willfulness is stubbornly digging in your heels about what you want or what you believe to be right. When you're in a willful state of mind, your focus tends to be only on your own needs and desires. It can be difficult to zoom out and consider the big picture of what's going on around you, your long-term goals, or what may be a more effective choice. You want what you want, and you will try to get it at all costs, even if there is plenty of evidence telling you to change course and do something different. Willfulness is rigidity.

On the other hand, there is a choice to be willing. Willingness is "doing just what is needed, in each situation, wholeheartedly, without dragging your feet" (Linehan 2015, p.346). When you are willing, you are open to the possibilities around you without clinging to the outcome you were hoping for. You are able to easily adapt and adjust in the moment. To sum it up in a word, willingness is synonymous with flexibility. In order to practice willingness, it's important to turn to the foundational skills of wise mind and mindfulness. Willingness requires you to be present; it's going to be difficult to act with awareness if your attention is elsewhere. Mindfulness brings you into the present moment, and wise mind helps guide you to consider all sides of a situation. Without making decisions based purely on emotion or logic alone, wise mind helps you consider both your emotional desires and the reality of what's before you to determine your next steps.

Let's break down the situations listed above to show the difference between a willful and willing approach.

TRAFFIC DURING A COMMUTE

Willful approach: Complain about the traffic; honk your horn; be critical of yourself for not leaving the house on time; find fault in others for causing the traffic.

Willing approach: Turn on music and sing along; look at the scenery around you while you sit in traffic; appreciate when people allow you to merge over; tell yourself, "I'll get there when I get there."

PARTNER DIDN'T DO THE DISHES

Willful approach: Do them yourself without saying a word, making a lot of noise in the kitchen; be sullen and distant from your partner the rest of the night to show them you're unhappy; refuse to take out the trash or do other tasks around the house in retaliation; let the dishes build up for days until your partner finally does them.

Willing approach: Do them yourself without resentment; directly ask your partner to do them using DEAR MAN (see Chapter 19).

RAIN WHEN YOU WANTED TO GO FOR A WALK

Willful approach: Tell yourself there's no point in going for a walk and sulk; refuse to find another alternative for how to fill your time; complain about the weather to others.

Willing approach: Put on a jacket and go for the walk anyway; find an indoor activity you enjoy doing; tell yourself you can go for a walk another day and it's okay to do something else today.

Cultivating willingness takes intentional practice, especially if you have current or past people in your life (like your parents) who were often willful when faced with unexpected challenges. In the tips sections, we will walk you through our own examples of willfulness and how we practice willingness ourselves.

KATE'S TIPS

This is a skill I love to hate and hate to love. I think it's great and useful when I'm in a willing state already, but I think it's awful and I don't want to do it when I'm in a willful state (which demonstrates willfulness perfectly, right?). When I'm in a willful state, for me it absolutely presents like being a sullen teenager, with a dose of toddler thrown in for good measure. Whether literal or metaphorical (it can go either way), it involves a lot of arms crossed over my chest, eye rolling, and saying or thinking, "Whatever" and "I don't wanna!" It's not a comfortable place to be emotionally, and it certainly makes me unpleasant to be around.

For me, willfulness shows up around emotional states. I am prone to clinging to my unhappiness. Maybe I don't want to move on because I think the person who upset me needs to really *see* just how much they upset me, or because I want them to feel bad, or not get what they want from me or the situation. Maybe I cling because I think if I get over something too quickly, it invalidates the emotions I'm feeling. When I get unhappy (especially if I'm unhappy because of something someone else did), I'm prone to actively trying to stay in that state. I become inflexible and rigid in my emotional state, rather than allowing my emotions to change without clinging. So, how do I get into a willing state from here?

Tip 1: Notice

Like with so many other things, the first step is noticing where I am in the first place. It can be a struggle for me to notice when I'm in a willful state. What helps me is really understanding what willfulness looks like for me, and what situations it most commonly shows up in. I recommend (when *not* in a willful state) sitting down and thinking of times you've been willful. Try to see what those times have in common. Try to remember what it felt like in your body, what kind of things you were thinking, or if the stimuli that tipped you into a willful place were similar in each one. The more you build your awareness of how and when willfulness shows up for you, the faster you'll notice when you end up in a willful space in the future.

Tip 2: Realize I'm mostly hurting myself

Once I've noticed I'm in a willful place in my head, the next step for me on the path to willingness is realizing that I am mostly hurting myself. It's very unlikely that clinging to my bad mood is actually communicating effectively with whoever upset me (turns out talking works a lot better). Staying in the bad mood doesn't actually have any bearing on the validity or reality of the emotions I'm having. Staying in a bad mood only means I am suffering more and for longer. Allowing myself to move on from my emotions will actually help me communicate more clearly with those around me. Moving through the emotions is also healthier and less painful. Once I notice I'm being willful, mostly just causing myself more suffering and not achieving any of my other "goals," I find it much easier to shift from a space of willfulness into a space of willingness. Try asking yourself what the *actual* impacts are of your willful actions.

Tip 3: Distraction

One of the most effective tools I use for getting out of a willful headspace is to distract myself. It's best if it's with something that elicits a very different emotion from the one I was mired in (this is using the E from ACCEPTS). I do an activity that is engrossing and evokes a new emotional state, like watching stand-up comedy or horror, reading a favorite book, or baking. I might also use opposite action, which might look like trying to pleasantly engage with the person who upset me. Once I've knocked loose the stuck emotion, I find it much easier to return to a place of being flexible, in the moment, and willing to go with the flow again.

MICHELLE'S TIPS

I have struggled with willfulness for most of my life because I am often busy with appointments, chores, emails, and more. I have a habit of trying to do too much with not enough time. I conceptualize this as being like Jenga. In the game of Jenga, you take wooden blocks and build a tower as tall as you can. One by one, you remove the blocks, hoping the tower stays standing for as long as possible. Most days of my life, I construct a plan. I decide what I want to get done and when I want to do it. Some days, everything works out perfectly, but those days are the exception, not the rule. Most days, something happens I don't expect. I get a phone call that needs my attention when I'm in the middle of something important. The lines at the grocery store take longer than expected, or a friend shows up late to the lunch we planned. All of a sudden, my picture-perfect plans aren't working anymore. Just like when you remove that one block from the Jenga tower and it collapses, so too would my schedule collapse around me with a ripple effect. If one thing didn't go according to plan, I would tell myself my day was ruined. I would get upset and blame other people for their incompetence. I would tell myself in frustration, "Why can't everything just go how it's supposed to?" In other words, I cling tightly to control and how I think things should be. I'm not in the flow of life, and I struggle to let go so I can adapt and become more willing.

Thank goodness for my therapist who has helped me move towards willingness over the years. I have learned a few things from her I will share with you. If you're a type A, driven, perfectionistic person, listen up! You're who I'm talking to because we are the people often most guilty of willfulness. This is how I've slowly shifted to a more willing stance.

Tip 1: Allow wiggle room

We live in a fast-paced culture that is constantly moving. We're told the more we can do, the better. At a certain point, I told myself to stop scheduling so many things in a day because it was creating the dynamic I described of needing everything to go perfectly or else. I now try to limit myself to only one big thing a day (i.e. one get-together with a friend, one doctor's appointment, etc.). This means I can be more in the moment when I'm there without watching the clock, hoping I'll have time to get to the next thing. It has greatly reduced my stress.

Tip 2: Take a deep breath

When things start to not go how you wish they would, close your eyes for just a moment and take a deep breath. It's more powerful and needed than you think.

This is a beautiful time to tell yourself the world isn't going to end, you can figure out what to do next, and it's going to turn out just how it's meant to (even if that's different than how you originally saw it going).

Tip 3: Put it off until tomorrow

Most things do not need to get done right now. I understand the temptation to accomplish things as quickly as possible, because I try to do that regularly. This leads to feelings of resentment, frustration, and shame over how long my to-do list is and questioning why I can't get it done in the timeframe I set for myself. Thankfully, I've learned what to do: make the to-do list shorter, accept what I can realistically do, and get to the rest another day. It's much better to accept your limitations than to push yourself and get upset when you can't do it all.

Tip 4: Accept help

Accepting help is a great way to practice willingness. We all have limitations, and no one has all the answers. You can choose to keep trying it over and over on your own without success, or you can let someone else do it on the first try if it's more in their wheelhouse. It may not be perfect or how you would do it, but that's okay. You likely just saved yourself a lot of time while connecting with someone in your life who probably felt valued because you wanted their help.

Tip 5: Remind yourself you're human

It's okay to not be perfect. Willfulness tells you to push until something is as good as it can be. Willingness says it's okay to just do your best and know when to stop. When I'm in a willful state of mind, I become critical of myself and others. When I'm in a place of willingness, I am more accepting and understanding of what I can and can't do. It takes a lot of pressure off to tell myself I'm human in moments of struggle.

PITFALLS

Pitfall 1

Like many skills, **it is tempting to think that the switch from being willful to willing will happen instantaneously.** Just realize you're being willful, decide to change to willing, and voilà! No more willfulness. Sadly, it rarely works that way. While your mileage may vary, it can take several minutes to make the switch. Even after managing to move into a more willing headspace, you may sometimes need to make course corrections in order to stay there. It is easy to slip back into a willful state of mind! So, when you try this skill, be ready for it to take a little while, and to course correct as needed. Pro tip: noticing that you're slipping back into a willful state is easier to catch if you're already practicing mindfulness of emotions.

Pitfall 2

When you're actively trying to shift your emotional and/or mental state, **you may be tempted to be hard on yourself for being willful in the first place.** Try to remember that the willfulness came from somewhere. Maybe the situation reminds you of painful memories from your past, it's a response to being triggered, or it's because of a strained relationship. There are hundreds of reasons one might be willful. Even if these feelings don't fit the facts, and even if it makes sense to shift away from them, that doesn't mean it's a good idea to be hard on yourself for feeling this way. In fact, if you are a dick to yourself about it, it's going to be more difficult to shift. So, once you've noticed you are in a willful headspace, begin by validating where you are. Once you've done that, then it's time to work on being willing.

Pitfall 3

Correctly labeling willfulness can be difficult. Most commonly, **boundary-setting is confused with willfulness**. If other people perceive your boundary-setting as willfulness, that can lead to questioning yourself ("Is my boundary valid or am I just being willful?"). Many people misinterpret boundaries as someone being unreasonable, stubborn, or petulant. This is where mindfulness and wise mind come in handy. If you're unsure whether you're actually being willful, take a few minutes to practice mindfulness of emotions or check in with your wise mind. It would feel terrible, and certainly would not serve its intended purpose, to try to override your own boundaries due to mislabeling them as willfulness. Don't discard your boundaries just because other people misunderstand them.

BENEFITS

Benefit 1

Willingness helps you stay open to new possibilities. When you are being willful, you are often convinced there is only "one way" (one right way to do something, one right outcome, one right opinion, etc.). You then become single-mindedly focused on doing a task in only one manner, making sure you get the result you want, or arguing your points into the ground. There is no way to grow or change without first turning the mind towards willingness and being open to other possibilities. **Taking a willing approach to life allows you to take in new information and consider other outcomes you may have first initially labeled as "bad" or "wrong."** When you are willing, you let go of your ego and need to be "right." Instead, you access your wise mind and look freshly at options before you to decide what will be most effective. Being able to consider other outcomes is only possible with willingness.

Benefit 2

Willingness connects you with others. Willingness helps you recognize your limitations; we all have strengths, and we all have weaknesses. Willfulness wants you to believe you can do anything if you only try hard enough. While there can be value in persistence, there can also be a lot of hardship in not knowing when to stop and ask for help. Willingness helps you connect with others in two ways. First, you are more likely to seek help from others and allow their strengths to fill in where your weaknesses get you stuck. Second, a willing attitude helps you go along with what others may want to do instead of pushing for things to go your way without regard for what others are wanting. The narrow-minded nature of willfulness can really create division and misunderstanding in relationships; a willful person leaves those around them feeling left out and unheard. **A willing person invites in other opinions, perspectives, and talents, focusing on what will benefit themselves *and* others simultaneously.**

Benefit 3

Willingness is the antidote to fear. Linehan (2015) says, "When willfulness is immovable, ask, 'What's the threat?'" (p.346). Underneath willfulness is fear about what will happen if you are not in control. If things aren't going according to your plans, you tell yourself the only other alternative is that it falls apart. Letting go of control and trusting others and/or the universe is no easy task. **Once you truly shift into willingness, you come to see there's not as much to fear as you once thought.** The next time something unexpected or unwanted happens, do your best to welcome it, just as it is, even if you dislike it. Willingness helps you recognize there is not as much to fear when you are in the passenger seat of life as you might think.

EXERCISE

Thinking about willingness vs. willfulness, can you think of a time you were willful? Give a brief description of what happened.

Can you think of a time you were willing? Give a brief description of what happened.

In your current life circumstances, where do you see yourself being able to use this skill the most?

Chapter 12

STOP

ABOUT THIS SKILL

We all understand that the word "stop" usually means to discontinue, end, or quit something. Despite understanding the meaning of the word, actually getting ourselves to stop what we're doing can be quite the feat. Compared to some of the other acronyms in the distress tolerance module, this one is much shorter. It's also a "step-by-step" acronym rather than a "buffet" acronym. With ACCEPTS and IMPROVE, you can pick and choose to do as many of the letters as you want in whatever order you like, but STOP is composed of four steps that are meant to be completed in order. It's a quick skill, but one that can be very difficult to do in a moment of heightened stress.

The STOP skill is intended to help with preventing poor decision-making before you do things that could really get you into trouble later. Specifically, it's a good skill to use if you're on the verge of a relapse with substances, about to get into a physical/verbal altercation with someone, or feel a panic attack coming on. DBT considers STOP to be a crisis survival skill (Linehan 2015), meaning it's a skill to use when you are in extreme emotional distress (think about feeling somewhere between an 8 to 10 on a 1 to 10 scale). We believe STOP is a wonderful first skill to use when you are experiencing an intense emotion. After you use this skill, you can then use other skills if you need to (such as check the facts, willingness, or any of the interpersonal effectiveness skills). STOP is intended to calm your nervous system so you can act skillfully and use your wise mind.

STOP

Yes, you read that correctly that the "S" from STOP stands for stop. Sounds simple, right? On paper, it is. The first step is to literally, physically stop what you are doing or saying. If that means pausing mid-sentence with something you started to say, that's what you do. In order to be aware of needing to use STOP, this requires an amount of self-awareness around how you're feeling physically in your body to know when you are about to head down a path you don't want to go down. Stopping what you're doing is the necessary first step to make a different decision. It may help here to literally think the word "Stop!" in your mind to help your body physically follow suit.

TAKE A STEP BACK

"Walking away" is perhaps the most common stress management strategy recommended, especially with anger. The best way to do this is to physically remove yourself from the place you're in: step away from the conversation that's starting to escalate, go for a walk around the block, or go for a quick drive. If physically taking a step back is not possible, take a mental step back. Imagine a lens zooming out from what's going on and see yourself and your actions from a third-person point of view. Remind yourself of what your goals are and see if you can "see the forest, not the trees." You can also take a few deeper breaths here to help you slow down.

OBSERVE

It's now time to bring in some mindfulness skills. If you have literally stepped away, you may need to do some observation of what is around you to help you feel more grounded and present. Practice naming what you can observe with your five senses or count your breaths as you breathe in and out. In addition to observing the environment you're in, you can also observe what you're thinking and feeling. Observing may take a few minutes, or it may take a few hours before you've had time to process what you're thinking and feeling. You can choose to journal here or talk about the situation with a trusted other to help you sort through your thoughts and emotions. This is an opportunity to practice dialectics by putting yourself in another person's shoes (if someone else is involved) and seeing if you can find a way to understand and empathize with them.

PROCEED MINDFULLY

After you've taken the time to observe, make a wise-mind decision about what to do next. It's likely your experience shifted (even slightly) while you were taking that step back to observe. Perhaps you are now thinking about the situation in a new way than before, or you are having second thoughts about what you initially wanted to say or do. Return to where you left off (if you can) and come back with a clearer mind. Make amends or acknowledge another person's point of view (if needed) and take a step forward towards an outcome that will serve you.

KATE'S TIPS

Though there are four different parts to STOP, I think the most important part is the last step of proceeding *mindfully*. If you've done the other three steps first but miss this last one, you're back to square one, and the skill won't work. Because of this, you'll notice that all of my tips center around the theme of mindfulness so you can do the last step to the best of your ability.

Tip 1: But first, mindfulness

When I think about this skill, I think about the importance of mindfulness and knowing yourself. In order to stop, you have to first realize that stopping is a good idea. You need to know your own warning signs and be mindful enough to notice when those signs are happening. When I get really flooded, one of my signs is a flat affect (my face looks blank). Now let's say I'm in conflict with a family member, and I start to get that flat affect. If I'm being mindful and present, I'll be able to notice it happening, and choose to stop and walk away from the conflict. If I'm dissociated on the other hand, I won't notice that my affect is starting to go flat, and I won't know it's a good time to stop and walk away.

Tip 2: Rewind and notice

Start by thinking back to past times when you were flooded. Can you remember how that felt in your body? Were there any changes to your posture, tone, vocabulary, or volume at that time? Was there a sudden or definite shift in your thinking or self-talk? You can also ask yourself these questions right after there's an incident of being flooded if you struggle to remember these sorts of things from your history. If you absolutely cannot think of anything yourself, ask someone you trust to tell you what signs they've noticed. Are there things they see that consistently happen when you're flooded? Be sure the person you ask is someone very safe whom you really trust, as this is a vulnerable question.

Tip 3: Know your signs

Practice STOP during minor distressing incidents so you will be better prepared to be mindful during unpleasant emotions/situations. Once you've identified some of your signs, focus on being mindful of them. If your sign is something physical (faster heartbeat, sweating, etc.), prioritize being mindful of your body. If your sign is emotional or mental (racing thoughts, intense anger, etc.), prioritize mindfulness of your emotions or your thoughts. Whatever form of mindfulness is your favorite or your focus, be sure to practice it over and over. The more you do it, the more natural it will be to practice it even when you're flooded.

MICHELLE'S TIPS

I feel incredibly proud of my clients when they do STOP. This skill is the unsung hero of DBT, and even though it's in the distress tolerance module, it's a key first step to being able to regulate emotional responses, too. Changing course and not going down the path you've gone down before is something worth celebrating. I also know how disappointing it feels when you find yourself down that same path, despite your best efforts to do something different. My hope is that these three tips will help you the next time you're needing to use this skill.

Tip 1: Take a step back by taking a bathroom break

I've lost track of how many times I have recommended to clients that they practice STOP by taking a moment in the bathroom. While at first glance it may sound a little ridiculous, hear me out on this. Nearly every place you may find yourself (be it someone else's house or a public setting) has a bathroom. If you need a quiet moment to yourself to breathe, cry, or close your eyes, shut the door of the bathroom and give yourself the opportunity to do that. The other good thing about saying you need to go to the bathroom is that it's likely no one will argue with you. You may not have many other things you can say to get out of a stressful meeting you're in at work or to get some space from your partner without them following after you. Going to a bathroom gives you a moment alone that you can easily access from almost anywhere.

Tip 2: Observe by talking to yourself

Most of us have heard "if you talk to yourself, you must be crazy." This could not be further from the truth. Talking out loud helps you sort through what you're thinking and potentially come to new conclusions about what you're feeling. It is a healthy, normal way to process stress and feelings of overwhelm. Depending on where you're taking a step back, talking out loud to yourself may not make sense or feel like a comfortable thing to do (don't do it in public). Some great places to talk out loud include your car or in the shower, as both are private. If you can't talk out loud where you are, consider journaling a quick email to yourself and putting your thoughts in writing. Make every effort to do this from wise mind instead of emotion mind as you're processing.

Tip 3: Let go of the outcome as you proceed mindfully

A key tenet of mindfulness is allowing all sensations and experiences into your conscious awareness without filtering out those you dislike or which feel uncomfortable to you. If you take that concept and apply it to STOP, proceeding mindfully means being open to whatever may happen next without clinging to the outcome you desire. Finding peace of mind comes only when you let go of pushing for what you want. Do the best you can in the moment, make a skillful choice, and recognize things may then fall into place as you had hoped or they may go in a completely different direction. What matters is feeling good about how you chose to respond, regardless of what happens next.

PITFALLS
Pitfall 1

There are myriad reasons you might have for wanting to rush through this skill. Stepping away from an interaction with another person can feel rude or awkward. Or maybe you're eager to get through to the other side of the stressful situation you're in. Whatever the reason, we caution you against "proceeding" too quickly. Make sure you've really given the needed time to each step. Have you fully observed? Have you been able to find your wise mind? Has your nervous system calmed down enough? Do you feel like you're ready to go back into the stressful situation without falling right back into the same patterns? Let this skill take the time it takes. **Don't rush your way through it, as that's a tactic that's pretty likely to have a negative outcome.**

Pitfall 2

While rushing through this skill is one risk, another is lingering too long. **If you're someone who tends to overthink things, or if you're prone to getting into "what if" loops, there's a chance of getting stuck.** Most of the time, that means getting stuck in either the "observe" aspect of the skill, or right on the cusp of proceeding mindfully. Pay attention to whether you're going in circles in your thoughts, as that can be a sign you're stuck. If you know you are someone who is likely to overthink situations, pay special attention to yourself. Self-awareness is a huge boon to practicing this skill well.

Pitfall 3

Let's say you just practiced STOP, and it worked...kind of. Now you've returned to the situation you stepped away from, and you feel like you need to practice STOP again. And again. This is a good indication that STOP is not the right skill at this moment! **Maybe your emotions are too high to be really calmed by STOP,** and instead you need to practice TIPP to bring your emotions down a few pegs before you can effectively engage in other skills. Maybe you keep getting riled up because of a situation where FAST or DEAR MAN would help with boundary-setting or getting your needs met. The situation may be too big and enduring for STOP, and you need to look at longer-term distress tolerance skills. Whatever the case may be, if you're feeling the need to use the skill on repeat, that's a good reason to pause and consider if a different skill may be more effective for your current situation.

BENEFITS

Benefit 1

STOP provides a good foundation for intervening when your emotion mind is strong. Without pausing to take a step back from a stressful situation, you may find it difficult to not engage in problem behaviors or act on impulse. **Practicing STOP gives your wise mind a chance to take over and puts your emotion mind on the backburner.** While there are many other skills that give you an opportunity to step away when emotions start to feel too big (such as distracting with ACCEPTS), STOP is straightforward and practical in almost all circumstances, whereas other skills may not be as easy to implement.

Benefit 2

STOP stands out among other DBT skills as one that does not take much time to do. STOP can be done in 30 seconds or less if you're able to easily observe what's happening within you and make a mindful decision moving forward. While other skills like pros and cons and check the facts have their place, they all require considerably more time and preparation to do fully. Having a skill like STOP to do at a moment's notice and that is easy to understand compared to other skills (that may require worksheets or planning) is much more accessible.

Benefit 3

Most, if not all, of us have had moments of wishing we could take back something we just said that hurt someone we care about. It's a natural part of being human to act impulsively without reflecting first on the potential consequences of your actions, but if that happens too often, you make a real mess of your life and relationships. **Practicing STOP consistently in relationships with others can be a game-changer in helping you during moments of conflict.** Because the acronym is easy to remember and understand, it can be shared with those closest to you and you can let them know you will be using this skill in moments when you don't want to say or do something that could damage the relationship. You can even name the skill by saying, "I'm going to use STOP now" to signal that you are going to take a step back from what's happening and think about how to proceed mindfully. Most people appreciate seeing the effort it takes to remove yourself from a situation to prevent it from getting worse, especially if you return with a calmer demeanor and a willingness to work through the misunderstanding without escalating further.

EXERCISE

Is STOP a skill that you think will come easily to you? Why?

If there's one element of STOP that you think is most likely to trip you up in the moment, which is it? Why?

How often can you imagine yourself employing STOP in your life?

Chapter 13

TIPP

ABOUT THIS SKILL

There are moments in life when emotions overwhelm you very quickly. Something so unexpected and shocking happens that you literally can't think or make rational decisions. This is most commonly known as the "fight or flight" response. Research has now shown that there is a third option of "freeze," and some say a fourth option called "fawning" (focusing on another person's needs in an effort to prevent the situation from getting worse; Walker 2013). In DBT terms, this is called a "skills breakdown point." What this means is that you are in a state of crisis, and any skills you might have been using up until this point to manage your emotions have now gone out the window. When many people seek out DBT, they want answers for what to do and how to respond when they are completely overwhelmed. They may be experiencing panic attacks, flashbacks from posttraumatic stress disorder (PTSD), or extreme anger that may feel uncontrollable. The TIPP skill was created for moments exactly like those. This skill is purely body based. The different components of this skill don't take much time to see results and can be done nearly anywhere. You can pick any of the four components to practice (it's a buffet skill!), and, typically, you will notice your physiology returning to baseline (e.g. your heart rate returning to normal) after doing just one part of the skill (though you can choose to do more than one part until you start to feel a change). Using this skill can be a fantastic precursor to using other skills. Once your body has been calmed by using TIPP, you can then check the facts, access your wise mind, or use any other skill that seems appropriate to help you with the stressful situation you're currently in.

TEMPERATURE

The directions for using temperature effectively are very specific: hold your breath and put your face in a bowl of cold water (make sure the water is above 50 degrees Fahrenheit/10 degrees Celsius). Hold your face in the bowl of cold water (while holding your breath) for 30 seconds (Linehan 2015). Sounds pretty unpleasant, doesn't it? It's not meant to feel nice. Also, please don't do it if you have any kind of medical condition that may make this unsafe for you. Unpleasant though it may be, the truth is that it works very well in changing your physiology quickly. Intense anger or anxiety often lead to an increased heart rate and cortisol (the stress hormone) rushing through your body (Leggett et al. 2015). Using temperature in this way and activating our dive reflex stops that in its tracks (Lindholm and Lundgren 2008).

INTENSE EXERCISE

One of the many benefits of exercise is that it releases endorphins, the chemicals that make us feel good (Harper and Sutton 1984). By changing the chemistry in your brain, you shift your emotional experience. Moving your body satisfies physical urges that arise when experiencing fight or flight. Intense exercise tricks your body into thinking that it has expended the physical effort required to either flee or fight (Freishtat 2013). When it comes to using intense exercise, be mindful of your body's limitations. Do not exercise intensely for too long, even if you have the physical capability to do so. Exercise intensely for only five minutes at most (you may only need to do two to three minutes to feel the effect). Once you start to huff and puff or sweat, it's time to stop, even if you've only done it for 30 to 60 seconds. Options for intense exercise include going up and down stairs as fast as you can, jumping jacks, running, hitting a pillow, or any other aerobic activity that elevates your heart rate. In our groups, we have people clap as quickly as they can for only 15 to 30 seconds, and most people are typically breathing a little heavier after we do this without even needing to move their lower bodies.

PACED BREATHING

Breathing plays a huge role in how the rest of the body functions. If you're out of breath or breathing shallowly, every other system in your body starts over-functioning (like your heart beating faster). If you're breathing slowly (indicating to your brain that you're safe) your parasympathetic nervous system gets activated, and you start to feel calm (Gerritsen and Band 2018). With the first two components of TIPP, you might question how it would work to actually do those things in the moment. You may not be able to stick your face in a bowl of cold water at work, and you can't do jumping jacks if you're having a panic attack while driving, for example. Breathing, however, is a different story because your breath is always with you. You can change the way you breathe at any time, and no one will likely notice. There are many ways to practice paced breathing, but most ways involve counting. DBT encourages making your out-breath longer than your in-breath (Linehan 2015). It's ideal to make your out-breath twice as long as your in-breath, such as breathing in for four counts and out for eight counts (Gerritsen and Band 2018). Another popular method is square breathing: breathe in for four counts, hold for four counts, breathe out for four counts, and pause for four counts before you inhale again. The same way that temperature and intense exercise don't take very long, breathing is a quick intervention.

PAIRED MUSCLE RELAXATION

The body's natural urge when you feel a strong, action-oriented emotion (like anger) is to tense up, because your body is trying to prepare for action. While one option is to release that tension through intense exercise, another option is to intentionally relax your muscles. This is the logic behind how a stress ball works. When you squeeze the ball and release it, your muscles let go of the stress they were carrying. Paired muscle relaxation is an intentional process of tensing and relaxing your muscles throughout your body, one by one. As you release tension, you may notice you sigh and feel looser. This is your body starting to slow down physiologically and settle into a more relaxed, calm state of being. To do this, intentionally squeeze or tighten a part of your body and hold it for about five seconds (if you can) while you inhale. As you exhale, relax that body part as fully as possible while thinking the word "relax" in your mind. Then, wait 5 to 10 seconds before moving on to the next body part. Paired muscle relaxation can be done in great depth (tightening and releasing toes, then your entire foot, then your calves, then your thighs, etc.) or in a shorter format of just doing it with the large parts of your body (feet, legs, hands, arms, torso, and face/head). It doesn't matter what order you do it in, and you can skip parts of your body that may be in pain. Going through this process can be distracting, as you focus all of your attention on counting while holding and releasing tension, and it has the potential to leave you feeling quite relaxed at the end. Some people do this while lying in bed as a regular part of their bedtime routine to help them fall asleep.

KATE'S TIPS
Temperature

My tip for this aspect of the skill all boils down to one word: commit. While this skill can be practiced in a variety of ways (as Michelle will talk about in her tips section), those are mainly for use if you currently don't have access to doing the skill as intended (if you're out in public, you aren't going to be able to stick your face in a bowl of cold water). But if you're home (or somewhere else where this is possible), do yourself the favor of practicing the skill to the fullest extent. I can understand the temptation to just splash water on your face or put ice on your neck, but for most people that doesn't work as well. At least once, try going the whole way, and see how well it works for you. Personally, I need to go the whole nine yards if I want it to do much for me, but when I do, it's really amazing how well it works to slow my body and brain down and bring me back to baseline.

Intense exercise

I hate the word exercise. It brings up so much negative baggage for me (and many others) that I generally avoid it, talking instead about moving my body. I also think the word exercise is misleading for this skill; any intense physical activity will do, and it doesn't need to be traditional exercise. One of the other reasons I really lean into non-traditional movements for this is that I have an injured back and knee, which make many forms of exercise painful for me. So, my biggest tip here is to honor your body and find what works for you. Use your imagination. It's simply important that the activity be difficult for you, and that you be unable to continue the activity for very long, due to its intensity. If it makes your pulse race and your breathing quicken, then it's doing its job. We're trying to regulate emotions, not punish our bodies.

Paced breathing

Paced breathing is my favorite element of this skill, mostly because it is the most accessible one. I think having a crisis skill you can do anywhere, in front of anyone, and without any extra tools needed is incredibly important. Pursing your lips can help to slow your exhalation, as can pretending you're blowing on a hot beverage. This will help you control the flow of air to make sure you're not blowing out too fast or too hard as you exhale.

Paired muscle relaxation

This is my absolutely least favorite component of TIPP. Hell, it is one of my least favorite skills in all of DBT. Why, you ask? I have no idea. I don't have a good reason. I don't even have a bad reason. I just don't like it. I admit this mostly to show that DBT is going to land differently for everyone. There will almost surely be elements of DBT that you dislike as you learn all the skills. However. Even if it's my least favorite, there's still benefit to be found here. For me, this comes most easily in the form of stretching. While this isn't the intended form of this skill, it still checks many of the same boxes. Stretching tenses and deliberately releases your muscles, systematically, and it can really help to slow your body down and help bring it back to baseline. Stretching may not be where you turn in the height of an emergency, but for slightly less intense emotions, it can be a great go-to for finding equilibrium.

MICHELLE'S TIPS
Temperature

I'll be honest: I've never used temperature the way DBT recommends. One of the downsides to this part of TIPP, as we've mentioned, is that putting your face in a bowl of cold water can't always be done. The good news is there are many ways to "tweak" this skill and still get some benefit by using cold water in other ways. My personal favorite is to splash cold water on your face in the bathroom because we almost always have access to a bathroom if we need it. You can also put an ice pack on the back of your neck, forehead, or upper chest if you have one available to you at home or in your workplace. You can take a cold shower or drink some very cold water. Our bodies slow down when exposed to cold, and there are many ways to use temperature to regulate your emotional state, no matter where you may be.

Intense exercise

I love Kate's reminder that you don't have to do stereotypical forms of exercise to increase your heart rate and get energy moving through your body. The same way you won't always have access to a bowl of cold water, you won't always have access to a treadmill or stair climber. For me, I only enjoy exercising if it's to music. It doesn't feel like exercise even though my body is definitely working while I'm dancing. If you're the same way, put on some music and move for a song or two. I also recommend going for a brisk walk and pumping your arms as you walk quickly. You'll notice your heart rate increasing before you know it, no gym required.

Paced breathing

Ever heard of diaphragmatic breathing? It's what singers do to help control their breath and hold notes longer. This breathing is distinctly different from normal, everyday breathing which is shallow and uses more of your upper chest. Diaphragmatic breathing uses your stomach and brings more oxygen to your body. The goal behind paced breathing is to intentionally change the breath in a way that will activate the parasympathetic nervous system, and deepening the breath through diaphragmatic breathing is one way to do this. Though I appreciate and find it helpful to count the length of in-breaths and out-breaths, if you find it too distracting or frustrating, simply focus on noticing if you can make your stomach expand when you breathe in, regardless of how many counts you inhale or exhale for.

Paired muscle relaxation

Doing complete paired muscle relaxation as it is intended to be done is not always realistic. You will certainly draw attention if you do it fully around others, and it can't be easily done when you're in the middle of another task. It is okay to only "lightly" tighten and release your muscles or to only do it with some parts of your body that others won't notice, like tightening and releasing your shoulders, your stomach, or your feet. As was mentioned previously, some people even use progressive muscle relaxation as a tool to help them to wind down at bedtime. Make this realistic for you, and don't pressure yourself to tense and relax every part of your body.

PITFALLS
Pitfall 1

TIPP is a skill that requires commitment. **This skill is unlikely to work if you only try it half-heartedly.** Splashing tepid water on your face, doing a slow jog or stretches, doing paced breathing for only a few seconds, or only lightly contracting your muscles for paired muscle relaxation won't do enough to change your physiology. None of the components of this skill are terribly useful if they get too watered down. If there's an element or two you immediately dislike, skip those entirely to start with, and try one you think you'll really be able to throw yourself into. Remember, this skill is intended for use when you are at the absolute extreme of your emotions. Half-hearted isn't going to do much.

Pitfall 2

Another pitfall you might run into is **trying to use the skill in the wrong circumstances**. As just mentioned, this skill is meant to be used when you are in an emotional crisis. Each of the interventions is created with that context in mind. If you use TIPP when you're feeling emotions at a much lower intensity, it's not going to have the same results. The skill may still be helpful in those circumstances (paced breathing, for example, can be utilized in a broad range of circumstances), it's just that it's less likely to provide the outcome you're looking for and may even result in you feeling worse. Before deciding to use TIPP, assess the level of your current emotions. If you're anywhere below a 7 out of 10, we suggest looking at other skills instead of using TIPP.

Pitfall 3

In contrast to the first pitfall, this one is all about overdoing the skill. All of the interventions in TIPP are meant to be relatively brief. You can't hold your breath in that cold water forever, it's not intense exercise if you can do it for an hour, and so on. **Some of the skill components could actually become unhealthy/unsafe if you do them for too long.** Also, if you've been doing paced breathing (or any element of the skill) for an hour and it hasn't helped...then it's probably not the right skill/component for what you're going through at that moment. When you approach using this skill, keep in mind that it is meant to be brief. If something isn't helping pretty quickly, then it's likely time to try another skill, for both your safety and success.

BENEFITS
Benefit 1

TIPP doesn't require much thinking, unlike many other DBT skills (such as check the facts and pros and cons) or other approaches to therapy (such as cognitive behavioral therapy). Just do the action assigned to each part of the skill (i.e. just put your face in the bowl of water, just do some jumping jacks, etc.) and your brain chemistry will naturally follow. So often in life when we are experiencing high-intensity stress, we try to problem-solve or think our way out of it. When we are experiencing an emotional crisis, this is not going to be effective. Under extreme emotional distress, your powers of reasoning disappear. **TIPP provides you with** short-term actions that do the work for you to change your perspective on a situation so you can then start to think more clearly.

Benefit 2

Speaking of short-term actions, **TIPP *quickly* returns your body to baseline**. When you have reached a skills breakdown point, you're in fight or flight mode; it's important to be able to get out of that state as soon as possible. When something unexpected or shocking happens to you, you may react in ways that don't serve you; you could make decisions that lead to bodily harm (purposefully or accidentally) or say and do things that damage your relationships with other people. It is essential to have a skill that doesn't take much time to intervene in these moments before you do something that could have devastating consequences. Luckily, with each part of TIPP you will see results in under five minutes.

Benefit 3

TIPP is good for your physical body as well as your mind. Because DBT is designed to treat mental health, the focus of each skill is on changing your thoughts or emotions to then choose a new, more effective behavior. However, TIPP is a skill that targets the body first and is bottom-up, meaning you do something with the body to change the mind (compared to a top-down approach, which focuses on changing what you're thinking or feeling first in order to then change the body). In general, the benefits of exercise are well known by most people as well as the benefits of breathing intentionally, but TIPP takes this a step further. When you are under duress, your brain starts releasing cortisol (the stress hormone). Too much cortisol can lead to high blood pressure, intestinal problems, a suppressed immune system, and more (Cay et al. 2018). **TIPP reduces the amount of cortisol released in your body.** When you're better able to return your body to baseline, you reduce the likelihood of experiencing the side effects associated with elevated levels of stress long term.

EXERCISE

Which element of this skill do you feel drawn to the most, and why?

Which part of TIPP do you like the least? Can you explain why?

Looking at TIPP, can you imagine it being useful to you in your life? Where/ how can you see yourself employing it the most?

PART 3

EMOTION REGULATION

Emotion regulation skills reduce the likelihood of experiencing overwhelming emotions and help you return to baseline when you do experience them. When your emotional experience shifts, the actions that follow are healthier and more in alignment with wise mind.

Chapter 14

PLEASE

ABOUT THIS SKILL

PLEASE is an acronym that describes the different elements of taking care of your physical body. It is our belief that the rest of the emotion regulation skills to follow will not be nearly as effective if you are not also practicing PLEASE. This skill is about more than doing self-care just for the sake of being physically well. You likely receive messages from your social circle and the media about what you are "supposed" to do to take care of your body (how much sleep to get, how often to exercise, what foods to eat, etc.). PLEASE looks closer at the relationship between physical well-being and how that impacts your emotional health in positive and negative ways.

TREAT **P**HYSICA**L** ILLNESS

When it comes to physical illness (or injuries) and mental health, there is a "chicken or the egg" dilemma. For some people, their physical illness or injury results in their mental health worsening as they start to enjoy activities less, lose concentration or motivation, and see their self-esteem decrease. For others, they experience mental health symptoms that then make them less likely to take care of existing health issues or which make some health issues more likely to develop, such as inflammatory bowel disease (IBS; Mudyanadzo et al. 2018). Regardless of which precedes the other, treating physical illness or injuries as directed by a medical professional can then lead to accompanying mental health symptoms improving. It is hard for anyone to communicate, make decisions with ease, and remain emotionally calm when in discomfort or pain. When the source of the pain is treated, all of those become easier to do.

BALANCE **E**ATING

In recent years, research has come to light about how food choices impact mental health (Lachance and Ramsey 2015). You are also impacted emotionally by how often you eat. The term "hangry" (feeling angry because of hunger) has become a popular term and accurately states that irritability is more likely if you haven't eaten recently (Bushman et al. 2014). If you are eating foods that don't have high nutritional content or you're not eating frequently enough, you are not giving your brain the fuel it needs to "think before you act" or to consider the long-term consequences of what you say or do before you emotionally respond to a situation you're in.

AVOID MOOD-ALTERING SUBSTANCES

Mood-altering substances include alcohol, drugs (illegal drugs as well as some prescription and over-the-counter medications), caffeine, sugar, and more. While everyone is impacted uniquely by different substances (one person becomes sad while drinking alcohol, while another becomes angry, for example), it is clear that using (or misusing) mood-altering substances does just that: they alter your mood. This may result in someone having a stronger or more impulsive emotional reaction when using a substance than they would when sober (e.g. when they are sober and feel angry, they yell; when they are intoxicated and angry, they destroy property or become violent in other ways).

BALANCE SLEEP

Poor sleep includes not getting enough sleep, having a hard time falling or staying asleep, and nightmares. Over time, the result of a lack of sleep can be debilitating physically and emotionally, as it becomes harder to process information and make decisions without sufficient sleep. The expression "waking up on the wrong side of the bed" illustrates perfectly how sleep impacts emotions: without quality sleep, a bad mood is more likely the following day (Scott, Webb and Rowse 2017).

GET EXERCISE

Physical movement has all kinds of positive benefits for mental health (Sharma, Madaan and Petty 2006). When exercising, blood flow increases and this has been proven to improve mood (hence the term "runner's high"). A lack of regular body movement can lead to depression (and depression often leads to not exercising regularly, which brings us back to the "chicken or the egg" dilemma). Studies show that exercise can powerfully calm the nervous system and lead to better emotional regulation when you are stressed (Anderson and Shivakumar 2013). It is important to note that you don't have to go to a gym or do typical "exercise" to receive mental health benefits from body movement. Move in whatever way your body enjoys moving with respect to what its limits may be.

KATE'S TIPS
Treat physical illness

This one has been historically difficult for me. Because of past traumas I am some-what dissociated from my body at baseline. I've argued about going to the hospital on two separate occasions when I needed emergency surgery. I also struggle at times with feeling like I'm "making a big deal out of nothing," which leads me to err on the side of minimizing. Luckily, I have been making conscious improvements here! I now try to err on the side of caution more than minimization, and to listen more quickly to folks when they tell me they think something is really wrong. However, I'm actually pretty good at taking care of myself for less severe issues (migraines, flus, colds, etc.). I am much more willing to tend to these ailments in a kind, present, and self-compassionate way.

What I recommend: learn what brings you back into your body. In the mindfulness chapters, we talked about observing and describing your internal landscape as a way of discovering what emotions you are feeling. It can be incredibly difficult to regulate your emotions if you're not noticing them in the first place. Illness, injury, and trauma can all cause you to try to spend less time being present with your body (sometimes reasonably so). If you have a rough time being in your body at baseline, or if you're prone to dissociation when ill or injured, be sure to have strategies for getting back into your body to help notice and regulate your feelings before they become overwhelmingly large.

Balance eating

My relationship with food has been a tumultuous thing. Much of my early adult life, my food choices were dictated by my food access (which is another way of saying I was stupendously broke, and so eating was catch as catch can). I was always *trying* to make sure vegetables and/or fruits made an appearance, but it wasn't always possible. I have also certainly engaged in disordered eating to achieve weight loss. Most recently, I've had mystery stomach issues for the past few years, making it so I'm often unable to eat due to nausea (which has, of course, entirely changed my relationship to food). These days, I'm mostly found eating whatever I think won't upset my stomach, while *still* striving to make sure I'm getting the nutrients I need. While I'm not one that notices much immediate emotional impact from eating or not, food as an idea and a relationship has impacted me considerably over the years.

What I recommend: think about your history with food. While some foods like sugar or caffeine may have immediate and physiological effects on your emotions, and lack of food can certainly make many people "hangry" (like Michelle talks about), another way food can impact your emotion regulation is your relationship with the whole concept of food or eating. If you grew up in a home that instilled a lot of shame or confusion around food, or if you've struggled with an eating disorder, even thinking about food in the first place may be triggering, let alone trying to actually eat. If you find you have an emotionally really difficult time even thinking about this aspect of the skill and how it impacts you, there's a chance that there's some painful history there, and that addressing that history could have a profound effect on the relationship between eating and your emotions.

Avoid mood-altering substances

I went from being incredibly straight-laced around anything other than alcohol, to some experimentation with illegal substances in my late 20s, to now barely ever drinking but using marijuana almost every day (due to the aforementioned near-constant nausea). That's a lot of changing! Through it all, one thing has been consistent: who I am around has a big impact on how often I partake in substances, and how much I partake in at any given time. Another common theme throughout these different stages is consuming more substances when overly stressed. For me, the things I need to look out for are who I'm around, why I'm using the substance, and how often I'm using it. Needing to use pot so frequently for nausea has actually been really upsetting for me, because I don't *like* using intoxicants every day, and I don't like the emotional numbing that seems to be a side effect. It can be hard to balance out my emotional needs/preferences with my physical health needs here.

What I recommend: there's no doubt that mood-altering substances do just that: alter your mood. So you don't have to wonder "if," or even necessarily "how" the substance is going to impact you in the moment. That said, I think the single most important question with regards to substances is "Why?" Why are you using it? What is the goal? Are you happy to be achieving your goal through the substance? *Will* you achieve your goal through the use of the substance? What are the downsides of using the substance for this reason? Get really curious with yourself, while trying to be as nonjudgmental as possible.

Balance sleep

Sometimes it feels as though I've lost the knack of sleeping well. I don't know the cause, but in the past 10 years or so, I just stopped consistently sleeping through the night. I started to have difficulty sleeping in, no matter how late I was up. Most recently, I've been struggling with falling asleep at a reasonable hour. It's infuriating! That said, I am incredibly grateful I am not someone who is ruined by too little sleep. Don't get me wrong, I prefer to feel well rested, and I certainly do *better* emotionally when I have enough sleep. However, I can actually function really very well for long spans of time with much, much less sleep than I would prefer. Considering how much I struggle to improve this one (though sleep hygiene helps a lot!), I'm grateful I'm not wrecked by being tired like some people.

What I recommend: in two words, I recommend sleep hygiene. Known to help you fall asleep and stay asleep, sleep hygiene is incredibly helpful. Sleep hygiene is all the things you can do to improve your rest before you even try to go to bed. For many, this might involve making big changes. However, you can often start small and still see big gains. If you struggle to get enough sleep, and you're one of the many, many people who are deeply impacted by a lack of sleep, I highly suggest looking at sleep hygiene. When you are looking for changes to make, focus on finding changes you believe you *can* make and maintain since consistency is key with sleep.

Get exercise

Of all the components of PLEASE, this is currently the most difficult for me. For much of my life, I didn't worry much about formally getting exercise, because I led an active enough life. I hiked, skied, and mountain biked and just naturally got enough movement. But, in the past eight years, I've suffered from injuries to both my back and my right knee that have entirely changed how I'm able to move and the activities I'm able to engage in. And that has been *hard* for me, emotionally. Since those injuries, I've not really figured out how to get enough movement in my life. I've been looking for the intersection between what I *can* do and what I *enjoy* doing, but that has proved elusive. This is also a place where I can improve my radical acceptance. The more fully I accept that I am disabled, the better I'll do at accommodating that fact in all arenas, including movement.

What I recommend: take the shame out! I suggest replacing the word "exercise" with "body movement" because using the word "exercise" may bring up feelings of guilt, shame, or obligation. None of those emotions are alluring, and none of them make you more likely to move your body. In fact, they make you less likely. Movement can be dancing, doing yard work, skiing, vacuuming, hiking...anything that uses your muscles and/or your cardiovascular system more than usual. There are myriad examples of the emotional benefits of moving your body. But you never get the chance to access those if shame prevents you from moving your body in the first place.

MICHELLE'S TIPS

Treat physical illness

I have gone into work when I've been sick more times than I care to count. I have to be seriously ill for me to take a day off. The impact this has on me emotionally? I criticize myself, saying I should be doing more to work through whatever illness or pain I'm feeling because I'm expecting myself to be at 100 percent. I am not very kind to myself when it comes to treating physical illness. Now I make an effort to remind myself the world won't end if I don't work for a day and to also do more to prevent illnesses from getting worse (e.g. drinking more water, taking ibuprofen at the first sign of a headache, etc.).

What I recommend: notice your self-talk around treating physical illnesses/injuries and the messages you received about this growing up. There is no need to be ashamed of taking care of yourself. Taking care of something now prevents it from getting worse, saving you stress and emotional turmoil in the long run.

Balance eating

For me to eat healthily, it requires preparation. I plan out meals for the week before I go to the store; this ensures I have the food I need on hand when the time comes to cook dinner. I slice up raw veggies at the beginning of the week to eat as part of my lunch, dividing them into individual plastic bags that are easy to grab. I also start to get "hangry" if I go more than five hours without eating, so I have granola bars on hand in my car and at my office. I am much more relaxed and at ease when I know I've prepared for my food needs.

What I recommend: reduce the likelihood of making emotion-based decisions about food by preparing nourishing foods in advance. If you are prone to going long stretches of time without eating, set alarms on your phone to remind you so you're keeping your body and mind fueled up.

Avoid mood-altering substances

Sugar is what I turn to when I've had a stressful day to give me a little bit of a break and a treat. While this is in no way bad or wrong, emotionally it helps me avoid or escape from what is causing me stress. What's causing me stress doesn't get solved by me eating ice cream or candy; it continues to sit there as I ignore it. I am served better by taking time to face what is causing me stress and determine if I can do anything about it before consuming sugar.

What I recommend: be aware of what substance you have as a "go-to" when you've had a hard day (and we all have one!). Find an activity to do instead to help you process what you're feeling that doesn't involve putting a substance into your body.

Balance sleep

In many ways, I do well with sleep. I go to sleep around the same time every night and sleep for at least seven hours. But this all changes when I have a lot on my "to-do list" to get done. I sacrifice sleep for the sake of finding more time to check things off my list by getting up earlier and earlier. I normally don't notice how this impacts me until a day or two later when I find I'm now more tired and not enjoying things as much as I typically would. While I do get more things done, I'm left worrying the whole time I do it.

What I recommend: trying to run on a lack of sleep doesn't work well for long and leaves you irritable with others and not functioning at your best. Prioritize getting the amount of sleep you need (whether that's 7 hours or 10) at all costs. You'll be able to get more done the next day when you're well rested.

Get exercise

When I was dancing ballet, I didn't think about how I was exercising for multiple hours a day; I was just doing what I loved! Exercise has to be fun or else I won't do it. I don't like walking on a treadmill; walking outside with a friend or my husband is much better. For me, I love doing Zumba® and swimming. I also pick a set day and time to exercise; if I don't do this, I am more prone to use the excuse that I "don't have time for it."

What I recommend: find a way to move your body that doesn't *feel* like exercise.

If you're not having fun, don't force yourself to do it. Make it a routine to fit body movement into your day, especially as something you do in the morning before work to get your day off to a good start. If you're having a hard day, moving your body can be the key to shifting your emotional experience.

PITFALLS
Pitfall 1
For many people, **there can be a tendency to think they can just skip over this skill entirely**. We understand the temptation. The links between your mental health and physical health can be subtle. Usually, we are all about taking what works for you from DBT and leaving what doesn't work behind, but PLEASE is an exception. Despite the fact that the links between your physical well-being and your emotional well-being may be difficult to see, they are very much still there. If you are physically run down, it just *is* going to be more difficult to regulate your emotions. So, even if you don't know how PLEASE will affect or help you, please (ha!) believe us that it will, and make sure you tend to all pieces of it to one degree or another.

Pitfall 2
PLEASE is a smorgasbord of subjects people like to shame themselves about. It is a sea of potential "should": "Eat right," "Don't do drugs," "Exercise at least 30 minutes a day," and so on. How often have most of us heard those messages? Because of things like that, **it can be incredibly easy to turn PLEASE into a platform for self-flagellation**. Remember, the goal of DBT is to help you suffer less, not give you tools with which to bully yourself. If you find yourself saying/thinking things like, "Oh, I really *should* go to the doctor," "I *shouldn't* have had dessert tonight," "I *should* know better than to drink coffee so close to bedtime," try to pause, and remember the actual intention behind this skill. Do your best to recenter yourself around some self-compassion before turning back to the skill.

Pitfall 3
People can sometimes make the mistake of **thinking the expectation with PLEASE is to be "good" at all five components of it.** If you've fallen into this pitfall, you may believe you've failed at using the skill when you realize there's always at least one component that's a *little* off. But it's not true! One reason introspection is so important for this skill is because it is nearly impossible to have all the elements going well at the same time. It becomes important to know which ones you struggle with most and which ones affect you the most when they are out of whack. That way, you know where to focus most of your energy, instead of spreading it equally between all five aspects of the skill. Conserve your efforts and spend them where they matter the most!

BENEFITS
Benefit 1
Someone attending to the elements of PLEASE can have a more satisfying life through taking care of their physical body in these ways than a person who doesn't. Going back to the "chicken or the egg" dilemma, **those who take care of their physical health experience greater emotional well-being and those who feel good emotionally are more likely to take care of their physical health** (Cohn et al. 2009). Taking care of your mental health often begins with taking care of your physical body. If your physical body is not being cared for (poor sleep, lack of body movement, unhealthy eating patterns, etc.), it becomes immensely more difficult to take care of your mental health and see changes in how you're thinking and feeling. Beginning with PLEASE sets you on the path to healing your mental health from past trauma or changing areas of your life causing you stress or dissatisfaction. Once you start working on those things, you may begin to experience changes in the present that will benefit you far into your future.

Benefit 2
Practicing all five elements of PLEASE is certainly not easy. It may feel somewhere between difficult and impossible to do all of this skill at once. But repetition is key here! The good news is when you establish a healthy habit, you set yourself up to practice at least one element of PLEASE on a regular basis with much more ease. Once you get in the habit of having easy-to-access healthy foods around when you're hungry or walking for 15 minutes daily, **it will then take less of your time and attention to make sure you're taking care of yourself in those ways**. When you don't make the time to do the elements of PLEASE, you suffer in the long run. When you do make a habit out of practicing PLEASE, it starts to feel easier over time to do those routines consistently.

Benefit 3
Though PLEASE is composed of five different elements of self-care, just focusing on one area impacts the other four. Let's say you want to start moving your body more often through exercise. Exercising during the day can result in more quality sleep at night (Kline 2014), and it can also help tend to a physical injury or chronic pain you may be experiencing if you're mindful about what kind of exercise you do. If you stop using a mood-altering substance, you may find you have more energy and desire to exercise and you may notice your sleep improves, too. You don't need to put too much pressure on yourself to overhaul your entire lifestyle to see benefits of practicing just one part of the skill. It's also important to keep in mind that the goal of PLEASE is to assist with emotion regulation. **Picking one piece of the skill to focus on may be all you need to do to see changes in how you're emotionally responding to stressful situations.**

EXERCISE

Which aspect of PLEASE comes most naturally to you, and which aspect do you struggle with the most?

_____

_____

_____

_____

_____

_____

_____

_____

Which element of PLEASE do you find has the biggest impact on your emotions? Can you explain why?

_____

_____

_____

_____

_____

_____

_____

_____

Where/how can you see yourself putting this skill to use in the next week?

_____

_____

_____

_____

_____

_____

_____

_____

_____

Chapter 15

ABC

ABOUT THIS SKILL

The purpose of ABC is twofold. First, this skill is meant for "reducing vulnerability to emotion mind" (Linehan 2015, p.247). In other words, doing ABC (either just one part of the skill or all of it) helps reduce the likelihood of making decisions from emotion mind. When this skill is practiced consistently, it will help keep you stabilized when stressful events happen. The second purpose of the skill is to help "build a life worth living" (Linehan 2015, p.252). When life is all about survival or reacting to things as they happen without feeling a sense of purpose or control, you'll be more likely to turn to unhealthy ways of coping. Creating a life worth living puts you in the driver's seat of spending your time in a meaningful way, and will help you feel capable of responding mindfully to life's challenges. You will build a foundation for your life that is purposeful and joyful, so stressors don't impact you as much. The "A" stands for accumulate positive emotions and is divided into two parts: accumulating positive emotions in the short term and the long term. The "B" stands for build mastery, and the "C" stands for cope ahead. Let's dive into each part of the skill in more depth.

ACCUMULATE POSITIVE EMOTIONS
Short term

Accumulating positive emotions in the short term consists of doing simple things that bring you joy. When you do something enjoyable for even five minutes, those experiences start to add up. Life is filled with work and things you need to do, but don't typically enjoy doing (like housework, going to doctor's appointments, paying bills, etc.). If your life becomes too consumed with tasks that feel like "work" with not enough "play," you set yourself up for stress and burnout. If you think of the expression "the straw that breaks the camel's back," life can often feel like you are carrying a million responsibilities or "straws." All it takes is one more thing, no matter how small, to go "wrong" (sitting in traffic, an unpleasant exchange with a stranger, losing something, etc.) to send you spiraling into emotion mind and feeling completely overwhelmed. Accumulating positive emotions in the short term does not prevent the "straws" from piling up, but turning to a short, simple activity you like can help you cope with stress and give a brief respite from it. Activities could include doodling, singing around the house, reading fiction, playing cards, and knitting (Linehan 2015). The time spent doing short-term activities can range from a couple of minutes to a couple of hours, depending on how much time you have available and want to devote to it. No matter how much time you spend doing a pleasant event, what matters most is doing it mindfully. This hopefully leaves you feeling energetically replenished and less stressed afterward.

Long term

What often leads to experiencing intense emotional responses to daily stressors is a deep-down dissatisfaction with the big picture of your life. Typically, you don't consciously think about this, but whether or not you are living life in alignment with your values influences how you move through the world. If you are living a full, meaningful life and spending your time doing things that matter to you, the little stressors that life brings your way won't throw you off as much. You'll be able to roll with the punches, be flexible, and use your wise mind because you have a stable foundation. If you're already unhappy with your circumstances, you are going to be more impacted by difficult events, even if they may be rather minor (in other words, you're already going to have a lot of "straws on your back" if you don't like your life very much). In order to create positive emotions long term, DBT believes you must first know your values. Examples of values include "achieving things in life," "having a life full of exciting events," "being self-directed," "contributing to the larger community," and working at "self-development" (Linehan 2015, pp.253–255). After identifying a value to work on, the next step is to determine a goal related to the value. For example, if your value is to contribute to the larger community, a goal for this value might be to find a place to volunteer. After deciding on a goal, the last step is to decide what specific action steps are needed to make that goal a reality and to pick an action step that can be done today. Action steps for finding a place to volunteer could include researching volunteer organizations online and completing a volunteer application for the one that interests you the most. Picking an action step that can be done today is crucial to doing this skill. Oftentimes, people know what they want to do, but they have a hard time actually doing what they value because it seems too out of reach. Even though the focus here is long term, the only way to get there is to start taking small steps as soon as possible to move in the right direction and prioritize your values.

BUILD MASTERY

It is a universal truth that as human beings we all have talents and skills, and we also all have weaknesses and flaws. It is impossible to be good at everything, and it's also impossible to be good at nothing. When you start to experience overwhelm in your life, it becomes far easier to notice your struggles than to notice your strengths.

Many times you are struggling in the first place because you are in a position of facing something you've never experienced before; you find yourself not knowing what to do and floundering as you try to figure it out. The antidote to this is building mastery. Building mastery is doing something you're already good at and feeling a sense of accomplishment, pride, and confidence after you do it. In the context of emotion regulation, your parasympathetic nervous system (our "rest and digest" response) gets activated when you are in your comfort zone (White 2008). Some people are in their comfort zone when they're reading a book because they love to read. Others are in their comfort zone when they're out on a field playing a sport they love or sitting at a piano playing a melody. Chances are the activities that lead to you feeling in your own personal comfort zone are things you feel competent at and enjoy doing. Every time you do that activity, you're building mastery of it and becoming better and more at ease, expanding your comfort zone as you take new steps to learn more and try new things in this area.

Building mastery is not about becoming a master or being "the best" at something. It is not about comparing yourself to other people or trying to beat them either. The purpose of doing something you feel good at is to bring you back home emotionally to your comfort zone where you can feel proud of yourself and be reminded of your strengths. At the end of a challenging day, it's about knowing you can do an activity that will bring you peace and confidence. It can be a helpful reminder when you're feeling overwhelmed by outside stressors that you have strengths and abilities. It also doesn't matter what it is that you're good at. Throw yourself into it without any judgment about whether it makes an impact to do the thing you're doing. Maybe you're really good at calligraphy: write something in calligraphy. If you're good at playing music or singing, play or sing a song that challenges you ever so slightly (but is also one you love). If you love to cook, cook your signature dish that evening for dinner. No matter what it is you choose to do, praise and appreciate yourself for the talents and abilities you hold.

COPE AHEAD

The final component of the ABC skill feels to us like a standalone skill in and of itself because of how much value it offers. It does much more than help someone find their wise mind and build a life worth living. Cope ahead is also a powerful tool to manage anxiety and to remind you what is within your control when facing difficult situations. Cope ahead consists of five steps (Linehan 2015). First, describe the situation you are worried about as objectively as possible. Be factual and make sure that emotion mind is not coloring your perception of that situation. Second, figure out how you want to cope with the situation. If it's a situation where you may typically find yourself engaging in a problem behavior, what alternative choices could you make instead? Third, start to imagine the situation. It's helpful to close your eyes when you do this and block out distractions. It is of the utmost importance to imagine the situation as realistically as possible. Based on what you do know about the place you'll be at and the people who may be there, think about events happening as they typically would. Imagine people you know acting as they usually do rather than imagining the situation as you want it to be. Fourth, start to imagine yourself coping well with the situation as stressful events or interactions may unfold. Be as clear and specific as you can with what you want to do and how you want to skillfully respond. The final step is to take some time to relax after you've done this exercise. Without this last step, it is all too easy to immediately move forward with your day and not fully integrate the mental work you just did to plan out coping effectively.

KATE'S TIPS
Accumulate positive emotions

Accumulating positive emotions is one of my favorites because I practice it frequently and the most instinctively. I have always been a person who notices the little things. I will stand for five minutes watching a little bird flit about or watching the shifting colors of a sunset. I will close my eyes and just savor an amazing bite of food. In short, I do my damnedest to mindfully attend to every small pleasure my world makes available, even if only for a moment. Obviously, I still miss many of them. Despite that, I think this trait does more to sustain my mental well-being than possibly any other.

When I teach this skill, I tell people to think of life as being a giant set of scales. On one side go all of your shitty experiences, and on the other side go all of your pleasant experiences. I then remind everyone that life will take care of making sure enough shitty things happen. You don't need to chase down suffering and sadness. They will find you. You couldn't prevent them if you tried. That said, one thing you *can* do is make sure you are adding good things to the other side of the scale in order to help balance out the shitty. Maybe it could even tip the scales in your favor.

Small things matter, and tiny pleasures count. If you've ever experienced severe depression, you know how hard it is to even consider trying to engage in grander pleasures. While grander pleasant events such as a vacation will certainly add a lot of weight to that side of the scale, you can add just as much weight there through a dozen smaller (and probably more accessible) things.

Build mastery

We are all good at *something*. Yes, you included. Maybe you're good at something considered impressive by most people. Maybe you're good at something so unusual most people don't know what it is. Maybe you're good at something utterly mundane, or even inane. I don't know what it is for you, but I know you're good at *something*. My favorite personal example is that I am incredibly good at making grilled cheese sandwiches. Are my sandwiches going to change the world? Certainly not. But it still feels good to make them for people because engaging in tasks where you feel competent feels really nice. And while doing things you already do well is great (definitely a mood and self-esteem booster), it may feel even better to be *getting* good at something. Picking up a new skill, practicing it, seeing your increasing ability...it's all just really, really helpful.

My biggest tip here is to remember that your skill doesn't have to be amazing. You don't have to be the best at the skill; you don't have to have a skill anyone but you appreciates as such. Build mastery is for *you*, not anyone else. The only opinion or experience that matters here is yours. So, go forth and make amazing grilled cheese...or whatever *your* special skill is. I bet you notice an improvement in your mood and your self-worth when you do it.

Cope ahead

The way I conceive of cope ahead is like using the power of your imagination for good instead of evil. I'm sure we're all quite used to using our imaginations for evil. I bet you have spent plenty of time imagining a dreaded upcoming event and imagining all the ways that dreaded event could go badly and all the ways you could fuck it up. This skill asks you to instead imagine that same dreaded event, but this time imagine yourself navigating the event skillfully and with even-keeled emotions. You can also think of this as rehearsing the event the same way race car drivers visualize themselves driving the track over and over in their heads as a way to practice. The more you *imagine* yourself doing a thing a particular way, the more likely you are to actually *do* the thing that way when the time comes (Blankert and Hamstra 2017).

The good news here is that this means you're much more likely to behave skillfully if you just imagine yourself being skillful over and over again. The bad news is that you've probably already spent a lot of time imagining yourself acting unskillfully! You've already increased your chances of unskilled behavior, so try to be kind to yourself. Changing your habitual behavior is hard! Just return to imagining your own skillful behavior again and again. Over time, you will build up and reinforce new habits. Remember that your imagination is actually very powerful at shaping how you behave, and harness that power to your advantage.

MICHELLE'S TIPS
Accumulate positive emotions

I often talk to clients I work with about zooming out or zooming in on their lives when they are feeling stressed, worried, or depressed. Some people feel like their life "looks good on paper." They have the dream existence with a career they love, a nice house, an overall happy marriage, and so on. However, they find themselves spending their time working constantly at their job or engaged in stressful activities during their free time. These people are drowning in their stress, and they're not taking the time to do short-term, pleasant events, even if they are living out their values through their work or other activities. I encourage them to "zoom in" on how they're spending their time and see where they can find even just 5 to 10 minutes to do something they enjoy. Other people may do well at enjoying themselves in their daily lives; they might spend their days with friends or have ample time to do small activities they like. But these folks feel empty, and like their life doesn't hold any real meaning. They tend to feel like they don't have a direction or like something is missing that they want strongly. With these clients, I ask them to "zoom out" and think about their values and let those guide them with what big changes might need to be made in their lives.

You absolutely need to accumulate positive emotions in both the short term and the long term to truly feel like you are leading a life worth living. For myself, I often neglect the short term. I get so caught up in trying to make sure the big picture of my life is what I want that I don't leave a lot of time or space to do something just for the enjoyment of it. It certainly is not easy to make time for pleasant events, and in order to do it consistently I have to schedule it in. If I don't commit to doing it, I'll bypass it when the time comes in favor of doing something more "productive." If you're like me, it's time to zoom in. Really look closely at how you're spending your days and decide if anything can be postponed or shifted to make space for more enjoyable, little things. If you initially tell yourself nothing can change, look again; I guarantee that there's a way to make space in your life for at least one pleasant event a day. Start with ten minutes somewhere. You can also do the mundane tasks of life in a more enjoyable way. Sing along to music while you cook dinner or while you drive. Close your eyes and take a deep breath when you drink your morning coffee or tea and savor it. Watch a movie you like as you fold the laundry. Over time, those small things start to add up in a positive way.

Build mastery

If you're a perfectionist like me, build mastery is both your friend and your enemy. On the one hand, if you're a perfectionist facing too many new tasks lately that you're stumbling through, you may need a reminder you're still good at *something* to help your bruised ego. On the other hand, a perfectionist's focus tends to be on being the best. It doesn't matter if you get an A; you want an A+. If you're trying to build mastery and internally criticizing yourself throughout the activity you chose, it's a sign you need to pause. The goal of this skill is to feel good about yourself at the end of it, to feel proud of what you did. You also want to have an experience of feeling less stressed, rather than more stressed because you didn't do that thing to your high standards. Ideally, building mastery helps you find a state of flow (Csikszentmihalyi 1990). For example, I love to do jigsaw puzzles, and I'm quite good at them. Sometimes I do puzzles that are really difficult and find myself having a headache after because I just spent 15 minutes trying to fit pieces together with no luck. Other times, the puzzle comes together easily for me, and I'm putting forth just the right amount of effort, finding that sweet spot where it's not too difficult or too easy. That's the spot to be in for building mastery. If I truly want to practice this skill, I am best served by taking a step back when I feel frustrated about a puzzle; that's not the experience I want to have. In these moments I could find an easier puzzle to work on instead so I regain my sense of mastery or lower my own standards in my head for how well I think I should be doing on it. Puzzles are my thing, but think about what your thing is and how you can create an experience of building mastery with it for yourself.

Cope ahead

I love cope ahead *and* I also don't do it how DBT recommends. I process best by putting words to my experience and talking through a plan rather than picturing a plan. I didn't realize for years that I was using cope ahead most of the time when driving to work or driving to a social get-together as a way to manage feelings of anxiety that were coming up for me. I would talk to myself while driving and find myself saying things like, "If they say ___ to me, then I'm just going to say ___ back" or "First, I'll get this form out of the way, then I'll respond to my emails, and then I'll start returning phone calls" as a way to map out what tasks I'd want to complete at work. Creating a plan like this helps me immensely, even when unexpected things come up I didn't prepare for. Coping ahead by talking out loud to myself (in the car, in the shower, etc.) has provided me with a compass over the years to know what direction I want to go in. Other people and outside factors may certainly lead to me needing to adapt and be flexible, but I have a home base to come back to with what I planned for originally. Thinking about it in my head (with or without imagery) or writing it down does not concretize my intentions as much as hearing myself say them out loud. Coping ahead helps me keep the focus on myself and my goals instead of getting caught up in what other people want. I have learned I can show up in a way that feels good to me, no matter what other people may decide to do, and that is all thanks to this skill. If you're not a visualizer either, that's okay. There are many ways to cope ahead.

PITFALLS
Pitfalls of accumulating positive emotions

You do not need to have big, positive things happen for this skill to be effective. For many people, there are momentous positive occasions from the past that stick out and form permanent positives that live on that side of the scale for life. However, **it's not realistic to expect or even hope for those big things to happen regularly; it's a slippery slope to rely on them for your day-to-day happiness**. They are a blessing, not a staple. Instead, focus on the kind of positive events you have control over. This can be done through intentionally engaging in more activities that bring you joy, through being mindfully present to the joys that already exist in your life, or by homing in on one of your values and bringing your life into alignment with that value. Cherish the big things when they come, and work towards them as you're able. But in the meantime, remember to fill the gaps with the tiny, everyday treasures in life.

Pitfalls of build mastery

While a good portion of the benefits that come from build mastery are based on feelings of competence, that doesn't mean you have to already be competent at a thing for it to count for this part of the skill. While everyone is good at *something*, that something doesn't have to be what you do for this. You can absolutely practice build mastery by picking up a brand-new activity, one you have no skill with whatsoever. Kate has a favorite sticker that says, "Have the courage to suck at something new." **Many people hold back on trying something new because they don't want to suck at it.** But if you want to get good at a thing you know nothing about? You need to suck at it first! And notice how really excellent it feels the first time you realize you suck a *little less* than when you started. Having no skill or experience with a thing is no reason not to use it for practicing build mastery.

Pitfalls of cope ahead

The most dangerous mistake you can make with cope ahead is imagining people acting "better" than they usually do. When you utilize cope ahead, you really want to imagine the setting (including other people) behaving as close to real/normal/expected as possible. If you're going to a family wedding and there's an aunt who always accosts you, don't imagine her suddenly deciding to leave you alone for once. Imagine her being her usual, invasive self. That way you have the opportunity to imagine how you'd like to interact with her/what skills you'd like to use, and work that into the "rehearsal" in your mind. **If you imagine everyone else being "good" then there's no space for you to practice your skills!**

BENEFITS
Benefits of accumulating positive emotions

More and more research in recent years has shown the importance of taking breaks (Coffeng et al. 2015). When you practice accumulating positive emotions in the short term, you are really talking about finding moments and opportunities to take a break from the grind of daily life and do something only for the sake of pleasure. Practicing accumulating positive emotions long term by leading a life that aligns with your values gives you the extraordinary benefit of creating purpose in your life. Few things are as important as that. **When you move through the world embracing your true self and what matters most to you, you may never know the full extent of the meaningful change you create.** Erick Erikson, a German psychologist, created a theory of development that involved eight stages. The final stage of life (older adulthood) focuses on whether you experience integrity or despair (Westerhof,

Bohlmeijer and McAdams 2017). Creating a life worth living makes it far more likely that you will feel satisfied with your choices at the end of your life.

Benefits of build mastery

Many, if not most, of us grew up where we did not receive the praise or unconditional love we were worthy of receiving. Whether that happened because of an overly critical parent or a parent who was absent, children often cross the threshold into adulthood without much confidence in who they are or what they can do. **The biggest benefit of building mastery is that it can counteract negative self-talk that was formed starting in childhood.** If you are prone to criticizing yourself or believing nothing you do is ever good enough, practice this skill on a consistent basis to prove yourself wrong. Regularly engaging with something you feel good about and have a natural propensity for starts to build new neural pathways in your brain. This then allows you to approach hard, unfamiliar tasks with more confidence. Doing this can help with healing that "inner child" part of you that didn't feel good enough.

Benefits of cope ahead

Practicing cope ahead is similar to an athlete visualizing their performance in advance of stepping on the field or court (Blankert and Hamstra 2017). You increase the likelihood of doing something successfully when you've practiced it, even just by imagining yourself doing it. That visualization strengthens the neural pathways in your brain and makes it more likely that you're going to recall information or follow through on the intention you set when the situation is actually happening. **Cope ahead can lead to a feeling of empowerment and preparedness that increases the chances of you using healthier coping strategies in the future.** As we both shared in our tips sections, you do not have to use visualization to reap the benefits of this skill. Those neural pathways are still being strengthened when you just think about acting skillfully.

EXERCISE

Considering accumulating positive emotions, what positive experience do you think would be easiest to add into your life?

Thinking about build mastery, what is one thing you're already pretty good at, one thing you're at least a little proud of?

Where can you imagine cope ahead being useful to you in your life? Where/how can you see yourself employing it the most?

Chapter 16

CHECK THE FACTS

ABOUT THIS SKILL

When it comes to emotion regulation, prevention is important; this is why skills like PLEASE and ABC exist. The purpose of those two skills is to help with preventing big emotional reactions from happening in the first place. The belief is that if you take care of your physical body (by being well rested, fed, etc.) and your emotional well-being (by engaging in pleasant events, building mastery, and coping ahead), your emotional responses to stress will be less overwhelming for you and those around you. But let's get real: you need skills for intervening when you are already feeling a big emotion. If you think of your emotions on a 1 to 10 scale, preventive skills are most helpful when you're at a 1 to 3 (with 1 being barely feeling the emotion and 10 being feeling the emotion as strongly as you can imagine). Check the facts and opposite action (the skill we're going to talk about in the next chapter) are most helpful when you're at a 4 to 6, and if you're at a 7 or higher, STOP, ride the wave, and TIPP are going to be the skills to go to first. With this framework in mind, check the facts is a key emotion regulation skill to use when you start to feel your emotions getting stronger or as a way to help you come back down from being in crisis after doing TIPP, ride the wave, and/or STOP.

Feelings are not facts. That said, to be clear, you *need* feelings. Emotions help you make quick decisions (especially the emotion of fear) and help you form social connections with other people. However, if you live in emotion mind all the time, you'll find yourself in trouble. Just because you feel a certain way about something doesn't make it true. Let's say you went to a movie, and you hated it. Does it mean the movie was truly bad? Perhaps. But it also may be that it just wasn't your cup of tea, even if it was a well-done film. Let's imagine you see a tiny spider on the wall and run out of the room in fear. Can the spider *actually* cause you harm? Is there really a reason to feel as much fear as you do? Most of the time, no. If you pause briefly to evaluate a situation, you often find that your initial emotional reaction was not in alignment with what was really happening. Check the facts regulates emotions by helping you understand why you're feeling what you're feeling and showing you the benefits of shifting *what* you're feeling or *how much* you're feeling it.

Check the facts is a series of six questions. The intention is to answer each question as honestly and objectively as possible and to really get curious about what's going on for you. The six questions to ask are (Linehan 2015, pp.285–286):

1. "What emotion do I want to change?"

2. "What is the prompting event for my emotional reaction?"

3. "What are my interpretations (thoughts, beliefs, etc.) about the facts?"

4. "Am I assuming a threat?"

5. "What's the catastrophe, even if the outcome I am worrying about does occur?"

6. "Does my emotion (or its intensity or duration) fit the facts?"

Let's walk through these six questions with the spider example from before:

1. *What emotion do I want to change?* Fear.

2. *What is the prompting event for my emotional reaction?* I saw a spider in the corner of my living room.

3. *What are my interpretations (thoughts, beliefs, etc.) about the facts?* I hate spiders, I'm scared to kill it because I don't want it to move towards me/crawl on me. Other interpretations: Even though I don't like spiders, I know they do good things by killing pest insects; I don't know if it will actually come towards me if I try to kill it/remove it from the house.

4. *Am I assuming a threat?* Yes, that it will crawl on me, bite me, or bite someone else. Likelihood that the threatening event will occur: It could happen, but I've never actually had a spider attack me when I've tried to kill one before. It's pretty unlikely.

5. *What's the catastrophe, even if the outcome I'm worrying about does occur?* That the spider will actually hurt me when I go to kill/remove it. Imagine coping: I've never been significantly hurt by a spider but if that happened, I would shake it off of me, and I'd seek medical attention if I was actually really hurt.

6. *Does my emotion (or its intensity or duration) fit the facts?* No. Even though I don't like spiders and feel scared to go near them, I don't think it will actually harm me. It's an unpleasant thing to be near them, but not something to really be afraid of.

Because it can be difficult to remember all six questions in order, DBT has a worksheet created for this skill, and it's recommended to write your answers down to help with processing your thoughts (Linehan 2015). Even if you don't remember all the questions, just thinking about one or two of them can shift your thinking in a more factual direction.

KATE'S TIPS
Tip 1: Identify your problem areas
If I'm perfectly honest, I'm prone to catastrophizing (not in all areas of my life necessarily, but very much when it comes to worrying about other people). If you're late and I haven't heard from you/can't reach you, my brain jumps immediately to assuming you are probably dead in a ditch somewhere. That's me going from 0 to 100 pretty quickly there, right? If you don't text back "fast enough," you probably hate me (again, a pretty big leap). Both of these are examples of my brain assuming a threat and running with it, without checking how reasonable that threat may be in the first place. These are perfect opportunities to check the facts! What are some areas of your life where you find you could especially utilize check the facts?

Tip 2: Find a shortcut question
While I strongly recommend working your way through all six questions a few times to get the feel of this skill, I use a single question when I'm unable to do the fuller version (due to time constraints, not having a worksheet on hand, etc.). I simply ask myself, "What do I actually *know*?" It is important to use the strictest definition for the word "know" when asking yourself this: not "What do I think?" or "What's my best guess based on my experiences?," or anything else. Only ask yourself what you really, totally, certainly *know*. For my first example above, the answer would be that I know you're not here when we agreed you'd be here, and I have not been able to reach you. For the second, all I know is that it has been an hour since I last received a response from you. That's it! Those are the only things I actually know.

Tip 3: Look for a new perspective
Looking at "what I know" vs. "what I am beginning to believe" gives me a good starting place to consider if there are any other possible interpretations. Maybe you are both late and unreachable because you left your phone at home and have turned back to go get it. Maybe you aren't responding to my text because you're in a work meeting, your pet made a huge mess, or you dropped your phone in the sink. Once I really look at what I know, it quickly becomes apparent what I *don't* know, and therefore what assumptions I am making. Once I start to see that there are plenty of other explanations for what could be going on, it usually calms me down quickly.

MICHELLE'S TIPS
Tip 1: Make the effective choice
The spider example in this chapter is inspired by my authentic fear of spiders. This is the example we share when we teach check the facts because it's so relatable (and ridiculous to think about how we're so scared of an animal usually so harmless).

The reality of check the facts is you will likely have to use it over and over again; it's not a skill you use one time and then never have to do again. I *still* feel scared every time I see a spider show up in my house. The goal of the skill is not to feel emotionless. It's not to shame you for your emotions or tell you the emotion is wrong or bad. It's a skill to help you get curious about why the emotion is there and help you choose what will best serve you. Does it serve me to go running out of my living room if I see a spider and hide in my bedroom the rest of the night? No. What serves me is taking this step to pause and remind myself of what my choices are and to gently tell myself that perhaps there isn't anything to fear. It serves me to go up to the spider and remove it in some way, even though I'm terrified the whole time.

Tip 2: Face your fears

For me, fear is the emotion for which I most commonly use check the facts. Almost any time I feel fear, I now pause and check in about what "threat" I'm assuming. Most of the time, what I fear is very unlikely to happen, and when I remind myself of that, I face my fears and things turn out okay. Chances are you have something that evokes fear for you the way spiders do for me. Maybe you're scared to go to a social gathering if you don't know anyone, or you're worried about making a big, necessary purchase. So much of the work I do with clients is helping them check the facts (even though I don't always label it as a DBT skill). Having trouble facing your fears, even after you've checked the facts? Don't worry. We talk all about that in the next chapter on opposite action.

Tip 3: Be loving to yourself as you check the facts

Another way I think of check the facts is as a healthy way to parent ourselves. Children fear all kinds of things that will not actually harm them (such as monsters under the bed). They also feel intense anger (about another child taking their toy or being told you won't buy them the toy they really want). Children need their parents to validate their feelings while also helping them make good decisions. Having a parent who tells a child to "suck it up" when they are upset or who doesn't provide emotional guidance leaves a child feeling lost and confused about what to do with the emotions they have. Parents "check the facts" for their children all the time in a way that is kind and loving without consciously realizing they're using this skill. How would you coach a child with the emotion they're feeling? Would you want them to do what their emotional impulses are telling them to do (yell at someone, run away and avoid a difficult situation, etc.)? Chances are you know a variety of healthy responses to stressful situations; you just easily forget them when you're *in* the situation. Be kind to yourself as you practice pausing and checking the facts. Accept you will make mistakes and still act from your emotion mind every once in a while, and keep trying anyway, the next opportunity you get.

PITFALLS
Pitfall 1
It can feel incredibly daunting to do the entire check the facts worksheet. **Going through each question step by step can be time consuming.** One way to combat this is to practice the skill far more often than needed with average day-to-day events. This gives you the opportunity to get familiar and comfortable with the skill in low-consequence situations, and really cement the steps in your memory. Once you've done this enough, you'll be able to go through the entire process step by step in your own mind much more quickly. Another solution is asking the question from Kate's tips section: "What do I actually *know*?" It's quick and dirty, but it will usually get you a decent way down the road of checking the facts, and it's great when you don't have the time or ability to go through the entire process.

Pitfall 2
So, what happens when you get to the end of checking the facts only to realize that your feelings and/or their intensity don't actually fit the facts? **For many people, the automatic response is to feel a sense of shame, guilt, or embarrassment.** Bring a heaping spoonful of self-compassion to the table here, plus a load of mindfulness/ wise mind. Most of the time, when someone is "overreacting" or having a seemingly inappropriate emotion, it's just a giant sign of an emotional wound or trauma. You had the reaction you had for very good reasons, even if it didn't match the present facts. Mindfulness (specifically being nonjudgmental and effective) can help with laying down your self-criticism, guilt, and shame.

Pitfall 3
One thing checking the facts asks is that you be objective in your reporting. That is no small feat, especially if you're really emotionally flooded at the time. If you are someone who struggles with this, there are a couple things you can try. First, if there's someone in your life you trust, you can run your responses past them, and see if they can help you revise your answers to be really objective. Another thing you can try is imagining telling the other person involved your interpretation. Do you imagine they would argue with anything you're saying? Then it probably isn't quite objective enough. The goal is to come down to facts that everyone can agree on.

BENEFITS
Benefit 1
When you go with a knee-jerk response that gets you into trouble, you then have to pick up the pieces later from what happened. Pausing to check the facts before you act prevents you from taking actions you might regret later. In a matter of seconds, you may say or do things when emotions run high that have a lasting impact on you or another person. **Checking the facts gives you an opportunity to**

make a decision that could lead to a better outcome. Once your initial emotional response subsides, you make room for wise mind to take over and call the shots. Checking the facts helps you get there and reduces the likelihood of carrying guilt or shame for things you may have said or done that don't reflect your true self or values.

Benefit 2

Checking the facts helps you rewire your brain—truly! If you grew up in a volatile, emotionally explosive household, you were likely not taught how to respond to stress in a way that wasn't based in emotion. In fact, if you did act calmly, you might have been told you were doing something wrong. If that applies to you, check the facts is an essential skill for you to learn and practice. **Practicing check the facts on a regular basis teaches your brain to notice what is a judgment/assumption (and we all have tons of those, no matter what!) and what is objective reality.** When you start to notice your interpretations and assumptions ("They were rude to me") and change them to be more factual ("They did not look at me when I walked in the door"), it forces your brain to slow down and examine the situation more closely. Your responses naturally change as your thoughts change from this practice. You still feel the emotion, but you'll be moving through the world in a different way because of this skill.

Benefit 3

We both firmly believe that **check the facts can be a skill that shows you when your emotions *do* fit the facts.** Growing up in an invalidating environment and receiving messages about emotions being "bad" or "wrong" can leave someone questioning everything they feel and often telling themselves they shouldn't feel the way they do. This simply isn't true. Your emotions exist for a reason, and there can be many reasons for why your emotion would fit the facts. It fits the facts to feel sad when someone dies. It fits the facts to feel angry when you experience a boundary violation. It fits the facts to feel fear when there is a threat to your safety. If you go through the questions and come out realizing your emotion (and the intensity of it) fits the facts, that doesn't mean you've done something wrong! We love when this conclusion is reached, and we see someone breathe a sigh of relief knowing they are not "crazy" for what they're feeling. We hope that using this skill helps you find more compassion for yourself and what you feel.

EXERCISE

Is there an aspect of check the facts that you think will come naturally or easily to you? Can you explain why?

What about check the facts do you find the most daunting? Why?

In what situation in your life can you see yourself employing check the facts the most?

Chapter 17

OPPOSITE ACTION

ABOUT THIS SKILL

Opposite action is a follow-up skill to check the facts. When you find that your emotion, and/or its intensity, does not fit the facts (or your emotion *does* fit the facts, but acting on it would be ineffective), opposite action is the skill to turn to. You are responding to the world around you at every moment, always feeling something emotionally, even if the emotion is very mild or difficult to notice. You are constantly having emotional reactions to events. The problem is you may occasionally have emotional reactions that do not match up with the facts of a situation or would be ineffective to act on. In the last chapter, we described an example of seeing a spider in your house. Even if there is a part of you that wants to run screaming out of the room and not come back for hours until the spider has left, this would be an over-the-top emotional response. What would make sense instead is to calmly approach the spider and try to remove it from the room in some way or to stay in the room with it there, knowing it likely will not harm you. If you take these actions (even though you are terrified of the spider), you are practicing opposite action.

In order to give a full overview of what opposite action is, go back to the beginning when an event occurred. A predictable order is followed with any event that happens to us, big or small:

something happens → you think something → you feel something
→ you do something

This process sometimes happens in a matter of milliseconds, and you will not always be consciously aware of your thoughts and feelings. Check the facts will help you notice what you're thinking and feeling. If you change your thinking, you then start to change how you feel, and therefore you likely respond in a different way. However, just because the emotion or how intense it is might change after checking the facts, this does not happen every time. You may still feel an emotion very strongly even after checking the facts *and that's okay*! What matters most is what you do with that emotion. You can feel anger about something someone said to you, but you decide whether you become physically violent towards the person or walk away. When you feel afraid of something (like a spider), you get to decide whether you face your fears or run from them. When you make a wise-mind choice not to have your actions dictated by your emotions, this is opposite action. It is an intentional decision to not act from your emotion mind and to choose a different course of action. Let's look at some other examples.

Example 1: Invited to a party where you don't know anyone

Thought: I won't have a good time, no one will like me

Emotion: Fear

Initial reaction (emotion mind): Stay home

Opposite action (wise mind): Go anyways and socialize with others as best you can

Example 2: Someone got a promotion you were hoping for

Thought: This isn't fair, they don't deserve it

Emotion: Envy

Initial reaction (emotion mind): Call out from work, quit your job, talk badly about the person who got the promotion

Opposite action (wise mind): Congratulate them, continue to show up and work hard, explore other promotion opportunities

Example 3: Made a mistake while doing a public-speaking event

Thought: I'm a failure

Emotion: Shame

Initial reaction (emotion mind): Walk off the stage, refuse future speaking engagements

Opposite action (wise mind): Keep going and finish the speech, make a small joke of the mistake

Example 4: Asked someone out on a date and they said no

Thought: I'll be single forever, I'm not good enough

Emotion: Sadness

Initial reaction (emotion mind): Stay home, delete online dating profile

Opposite action (wise mind): Hang out with a friend instead, continue pursuing connections with other people

In all of these examples, acting from emotion mind would not benefit you. It benefits you to keep going and face fears (when you are afraid of something that cannot actually hurt you). Is it uncomfortable and hard to do this? Absolutely. Yet it also serves you in the long run and leaves you with fewer regrets. Emotion mind often leads to impulsive decisions based on short-lived feelings. They may seem to make the most sense *in that moment* when you are *feeling that emotion*, but in an hour or a week you may feel something completely different, and you are left to live with the choice you made then.

We are going to talk about some specific ways to practice opposite action in our tips sections, but here are some general questions to ask yourself to help you determine what opposite action to take:

1. What is my initial, unfiltered gut reaction for what to do here?

2. When I check with my wise mind, does it tell me to do that or to make a different choice?

3. If I were to make a different choice, what would it be? What would be the opposite course of action from what I wanted to do at first?

KATE'S TIPS

If I find opposite action so useful, why is it so hard for me to use it? Well, my emotions tend to be pretty large. Opposite action, by definition, means doing something in direct opposition to what your emotions want you to do. That can be a really difficult thing to talk yourself into! I hope my tips help you if you find yourself struggling with the same things I do.

Tip 1: Start small

My best tip here is to practice the hell out of this skill at times when your emotions are small (nothing above a 5 on a 1 to 10 scale). This will help you get in the habit of using the skill, making it easier to access when your emotions are running high. It also provides you with a history of evidence that the skill actually works. This gives you leverage when you want to try the skill during more intense situations. You'll be able to tell yourself it has served you well in the past and is likely to serve you well in this moment, too.

Tip 2: Use it after the fact

I most commonly use opposite action in the wake of some upsetting situation or conflict. I'll reach a point where there's nothing more to be *done*, and everything is resolved...but I'm still emotionally in the same space. Continuing to act on those feelings, however, no longer serves me, which is why I need opposite action. You may need opposite action long after a situation is over so that your emotions don't continue to consume you.

Tip 3: Be patient

One metaphor I use about my own emotions is saying they are like a huge ship on the ocean: they have a lot of momentum, and it can take a good, *long* time for them to change course, especially if that's by a full 180 degrees. Opposite action is a really great way to help me behave in ways that serve me while I wait for my emotions to turn around. It also helps me change my emotional course and accomplish the feat much more quickly.

MICHELLE'S TIPS

Even though opposite action may be easy to understand conceptually, it is far harder to do in the moment. My hope is that sharing these three suggestions will help you use this skill with greater ease.

Tip 1: Notice your body first

We're not usually paying close attention, but emotions are felt in our bodies instead of in our brains (that's where thoughts live, but emotions live everywhere else; Nummenmaa et al. 2013). Most of the time we're too busy focusing on other things to notice (or care) what physical sensations we're experiencing in our bodies. Just last night I was feeling overwhelmed and nervous about something, and it was strong enough that I noticed a queasiness in my stomach. I also regularly notice emotions in my throat; it will feel really tight, and I typically feel this when I'm afraid of something (specifically, conflict with another person). So, why is it important to notice your body when you're talking about the skill of opposite action? If you can change what your body is feeling/doing, your brain will catch up to speed and your thoughts will likely start to shift, too. A great way to do this is to half-smile or do willing hands. Doing these two simple actions alone can lead to finding wise mind. If you're angry and feeling clenched up or hot, intentionally relax any part of your body that's holding tension. If you're feeling sadness or shame, notice how it feels to sit up a little straighter. If you're feeling nervous and fidgety, try to still your body and take deep breaths. This way of practicing opposite action can be powerful and work relatively quickly to set you on the path of making a different choice instead of going with your initial reaction.

Tip 2: Practice gratitude

Gratitude is more than just telling yourself to "look on the bright side" or saying "it's not so bad." The idea of dialectics is that there is more than one side to a story. Things are not *all bad* or *all good*; they are both. Emotion mind tends to catastrophize and notice what's going wrong or what you don't like. Though this is perfectly understandable, if you want to act opposite of your emotions, practicing gratitude is one way to do this. Find something to appreciate as an opposite action for sadness, envy, shame, fear, or anger. The goal is not to make the emotion go away or to invalidate why the emotion is there in the first place. The goal is that taking a quick moment to pause and appreciate something then leads to you having more compassion for yourself (if you're feeling sad or ashamed), another person (if you're envious or angry), or the world (if you're feeling afraid). You are not all bad, other people are not all bad, and the world isn't all bad either.

Tip 3: Is it actually scary?

It's a universal human experience to be afraid of things that are unlikely to actually hurt us. Your fears can hold you back from experiencing the fullness of life at times and from connecting with others. I try to pause and ask myself, "Is this actually scary?" Within that simple question, I am really asking myself a) what is the likelihood that what I'm afraid of will happen, b) is my physical or emotional well-being truly threatened here, and c) will I feel better if I can face this fear safely and come out the other side? If I can say yes to all of those questions, I go for it. This is just another way to check the facts that helps me make an opposite-action decision (to confront my fears instead of avoiding them). It's important to note that opposite action is not appropriate in situations where your safety may actually be at risk. It may also be hard to have an accurate sense of safety if you've experienced trauma. If you have a trauma history, only use opposite action for fears related to your trauma with clear direction and guidance from your therapist.

PITFALLS
Pitfall 1

Sometimes emotions are a muddled mess. You can be feeling a veritable melange of emotions, and sorting out what's what can be a difficult task! **Even if you do correctly identify your emotion, what if you choose an action that isn't really in opposition to that emotion?** If you've tried opposite action, and it simply isn't working, ask yourself these questions: Is it possible I've misidentified the emotion I'm trying to change? Did I choose the wrong opposite action for that emotion? Those two questions can do a lot to get this skill off the ground if you're struggling.

Pitfall 2

This is not a skill to half-ass. Say you've been invited to a party, but you have a lot of social anxiety and the thought of going scares you a lot. The action urge would be to turn down the invitation. Doing full opposite action would look like going to the party, being open to having a good time, and maybe even employing some cope ahead to give yourself the best chance of having fun. **Not doing opposite action all the way looks a lot like willfulness.** You could go to the party all the while thinking, "I'll go, but it's going to be terrible and I'm going to have an awful time." Then when you arrive, you avoid everyone there and hide away in another room. The lesson here would not be "Oh, I guess opposite action doesn't work. I went to the party, but still felt awful and had a bad time." The lesson here is that you need to fully commit to your opposite action if you want to see the results you're hoping for.

Pitfall 3

Sometimes people use opposite action at inappropriate times. It can be used as a tool of avoidance by leaning on this skill to change emotional states that feel unpleasant. For instance, say you're feeling terribly sad. You check the facts, and your emotion and its intensity fit the facts. There are no immediate demands on your time at the moment; you actually have the space and time for this emotion. That's not the right time for opposite action! When used at the wrong time, this tool can do more harm than good. **It can cheat you out of emotional experiences or even be used as a sort of self-punishment.** Before you do opposite action, be sure it's the right skill for the moment. Ask yourself why you want to use it, and be honest with yourself.

BENEFITS
Benefit 1

When you act on your emotions instead of practicing opposite action, sometimes you are left with a big mess to clean up later. You can be left with amends to make when you said or did things that hurt another person in the heat of the moment or with a more literal clean-up if property was destroyed or if responsibilities were avoided instead of faced. Making the choice to act opposite can very much benefit you in the long run. Though you will still experience stressful situations in your life (after all, you rarely have control over initial events that take place), **opposite action ensures you are not adding any more stress to what may already be hard or overwhelming in your life.**

Benefit 2

The feedback we hear from people when they practice opposite action is that they feel proud of themselves for responding differently than they had in the past when facing stress or conflict. This tends to be particularly true when facing fears. Imagine what would happen if you never did the things that frightened you; you would live in an isolated bubble. Fears are a natural, normal, even necessary part of life, but when you do the things you're scared of (try that new food, go say hello to that person, go on a big rollercoaster, etc.), you typically leave the experience glad that you tried and did it. **Even if an experience doesn't go well, you can still feel proud of yourself for making a change and going outside your comfort zone instead of listening to your fear.**

Benefit 3

Opposite action helps you break out of old, unhealthy patterns. Responding in new ways to stress and difficult emotions is challenging work. It is tempting to respond in the way you always have before, which can look like yelling or name-calling others when you're angry, avoiding responsibilities and isolating for days when you're depressed/sad, or running away from things that make you feel afraid/anxious. You don't want to stuff your emotions down and not feel them (reason mind), and you also don't want to blindly follow what they are telling you to do (emotion mind). If you grew up in a family filled with impulsivity and chaos, this is a whole new way of being. You may have even been praised for *not* being in your wise mind (saying what was on your mind, doing what you wanted, etc.). **The more you practice opposite action, the more your wise mind will help you put thought and intention behind your decisions and actions.**

EXERCISE

What emotion do you think you'll have the easiest time with when it comes to using opposite action? Why?

Conversely, what emotion do you think you'll have the hardest time using opposite action with? Why?

If you were to practice opposite action today, what might that look like? Where would you employ the skill?

Chapter 18

RIDE THE WAVE

ABOUT THIS SKILL

Ride the wave (also known as urge-surfing) combines work from mindfulness, emotion regulation, and distress tolerance. Riding the wave requires use of mindfulness skills to observe and describe the emotion and urge arising within you. It's a skill used when emotional distress is high (like other emotion-regulation skills), while also being used in many cases with the purpose of tolerating distress. While it's a commonly talked about DBT skill, there is very little direction that exists on *how* to do the skill. It is for these reasons that we believe ride the wave is more of a *concept* than a *skill* itself. Anytime an urge arises to do a problem behavior and you don't do it, you've likely practiced ride the wave in conjunction with other DBT skills to help you get there. At its core, ride the wave is about waiting for urges to pass, and trusting that with time, your urges will subside.

Some people decide to actively "be with" and process their emotions (talking about it with others, journaling, crying, hitting something safely, etc.). Others use distraction techniques and opposite action in an effort to "change the channel" of their thoughts so they don't think about their urges. Both ways to ride the wave are equally valid and okay. As long as you do not act on unhealthy urges that come up, you've done it!

Though unrelated to DBT, general adaptation syndrome (GAS) provides a good model of how we respond emotionally to stress and describes three stages (Selye 1950):

1. **Alarm reaction:** Initially, the sympathetic nervous system experiences fight/flight/freeze (or fawn) when faced with stress. Emotion mind tends to take over first as you try to assess what's going on. It is very difficult to access reason mind, and this is when you may start noticing unhealthy urges coming up for how to respond. If you imagine the urge like a wave, this is when it starts to rise.

2. **Resistance:** Now that your initial response has worn off, you may be left trying to pick up the pieces from the stress you just experienced. This is when you are likely the most vulnerable to acting on urges, and this stage often feels like the hardest. Whereas the alarm reaction stage is usually short

lived (a few minutes), the stage of resistance can last for hours. Assuming you didn't act on your urges during the alarm reaction stage, this is where you are now going to start riding the wave as you navigate trying to respond skillfully to the stressful event that happened. This is the peak of emotional intensity, similar to the crest (highest point) of a wave.

3. **Exhaustion:** After any kind of big stressful event, your body and mind need rest to recover. People often describe a feeling of "crashing" (just like a wave) after stressful situations get resolved, and this is also common with ride the wave. If you manage to successfully resist acting on your urge, you will probably feel fatigued afterwards, rather than proud of yourself or joyful. This is not a bad sign and is instead a natural indication that you made a new, different choice to which your body is now adjusting as it reaches a resolution.

Let's look at this with an example:

1. **Alarm reaction:** You receive a text from your partner saying they "want to talk." Your initial thought is thinking they may want to end the relationship. They say they want to see you tomorrow in person to have a conversation. You immediately notice an action urge to drive to their house in an effort to have the conversation now; you also notice an urge to drink alcohol.

2. **Resistance:** Ten minutes after you receive the text, you find yourself fighting the urge to drink at home alone. You decide to ride the wave by calling a friend and going for a long walk.

3. **Exhaustion:** After you get home from your walk an hour later, you feel past the urge to drink, but you don't feel like you have the energy to cook dinner. You decide to order some takeout and go to bed early that night.

KATE'S TIPS

Ride the wave is so *simple* (have an urge to do a thing, but don't do it), that it's tempting to assume it is also *easy* (which it is not). In my opinion, ride the wave is one of the harder skills in DBT. It is an exercise in mindfulness, self-awareness, and pure willpower. And the more intense the action urge, the more difficult this skill. As I've said previously, I've struggled a lot with self-harm, and that is the context in which I've used ride the wave the most. The first few times I attempted ride the wave to get to the other side of the urge to self-harm, I didn't succeed. Just *thinking* about using the skill felt like asking myself to perform magic. Because of that, I wouldn't even try. Really, it's not that the *skill* didn't succeed; it was that *I* didn't succeed in performing the skill. This is what eventually worked for me, in terms of the components I mentioned above: mindfulness, self-awareness, and willpower.

Tip 1: Mindfulness

When I say mindfulness, I specifically mean wise mind (though other forms of mindfulness are in the mix as well). Those times that I opted not to ride the wave of my urge to self-harm, I was firmly planted in my emotion mind. I was scared (terrified, really), angry, and willful. Self-harm is certainly not a wise-mind choice; I heard my emotion mind loud and clear, and I didn't allow my reason mind to get a word in edgewise. If I had, my reason mind would have told me that emotional responses look like waves and that all I needed to do was wait it out. Leaning on my reason mind more would have brought me to wise mind. I could have used self-soothing with the five senses to take tender care of my emotional self, too. That is why mindfulness is so important here. You need to bring emotions *and* reason to the table to successfully navigate this skill.

Tip 2: Self-awareness

It's common to not want to look at or explore this, because there can be shame or self-judgment with action urges. Be sure to muster self-compassion here. There's no shame in feelings or urges; we all have them. The truth is that riding the wave is much easier to do the earlier you catch your action urge, and that can only be done with self-awareness. The better you know yourself (your body's signals, changes in your thoughts, etc.), the better chance you have of noticing the action urge early. Catching it early doesn't always prevent the urge from getting intense, but you'll be more prepared for what's coming if it grows rather than feeling blindsided. Over time, you may start to see patterns and predict events in advance that could trigger your action urge, and this will help you be even more prepared to use your skills.

Tip 3: Willpower

In the end, no matter what skills you use in conjunction with ride the wave to help support you in the process, willpower is the only thing standing between you and acting on your urges. And that's hard! The good news is willpower functions very much like a muscle. Like a muscle, you can exercise your willpower in order to make it stronger. What might this look like? Each time you want to reach for your phone, delay picking it up by even 30 to 60 seconds. Really want to buy that thing in your online cart? Sit on it overnight before you click "buy." Craving that cigarette? Listen to your favorite song before you step out to take your smoke break. In short, *practice*. Start by practicing with situations that have little to no consequences. Do a little more each day. Challenge yourself to wait longer once you get comfortable. Easy to wait a minute to pick up your phone? Great! Now, wait three minutes. Next, try five. Just like a muscle, your ability to utilize your willpower effectively in harder situations will grow.

MICHELLE'S TIPS

As a therapist, one of the most common things clients need help with when they start therapy is resisting problem behaviors of some kind. They start therapy because they feel powerless to stop their urges, and this is starting to wreak havoc on their lives. These are the most common tips I share so they can ride the wave in the future.

Tip 1: Repetition may help

As Kate mentioned in her tips section, you can slowly build up to tolerating stress for longer and longer, but for now, focus on what's right in front of you and put those mindfulness skills to work. Especially in the aftermath of something truly traumatic (when you may really need to ride the wave for strong urges), time is going to move differently (in other words, five minutes may feel like an eternity). Focus on what's at your disposal right now that you can do, and keep doing that over and over again as many times as you need to while time passes. It may also help to avoid looking at the time while riding the wave and instead staying tuned in to notice when your urge starts to change.

Tip 2: Don't do it alone

I am a big fan of seeking out support from other people when you're in the midst of riding the wave. Go spend time with a trusted other in person if you can, call/ video chat with them, or keep in touch by text. This is the whole reason why it's important to have a sponsor if you're in a 12-step program for substance use, and it's why crisis lines exist. Reaching out to someone, especially during the alarm reaction stage, can be a game-changer in helping you not act on urges. You also don't have to talk about the stressful event itself if that doesn't feel helpful; if talking about other things will help get your mind off your urges and get through the stress you're feeling, that is completely okay to do.

Tip 3: Be proud of any progress

Ride the wave can sometimes feel like all-or-nothing: you either do it and successfully resist your urges, or you act on your urges and engage in a problem behavior. In my opinion, it isn't that black and white. Even if you do act on your urges, my hope is that you have a different experience with riding the wave. If you think of it like literal surfing, not every surfer rides a large wave perfectly every time into shore; sometimes, they fall off their board. What matters in those moments is if they stood up in the first place, and maybe even stayed on longer than before. That's what I want you to think about with this skill. If you would normally turn to self-harm immediately after a stressful event, but this time you waited a couple hours and tried out some other coping skills before doing it, that is a win. You still rode the wave!

PITFALLS

Pitfall 1

Ride the wave is typically used to help you avoid problem behaviors. To put it another way, if an action is going to harm you in some way, ride the wave is there to help you not engage in that action. **If you use ride the wave, and you end up giving in and engaging in the action anyway, then you (and/or the skill) failed, right?** Wrong! Let's imagine someone riding the wave for 20 minutes but in the end they do their problem behavior. The temptation might be to say they failed (or that ride the wave failed), but there's a dialectic to fall back on here. Yes, the goal is to avoid the problem behavior altogether. However, *any* movement in that direction (such as resisting for 20 minutes) is still a success! Try to avoid all or nothing, black-and-white thinking with this skill.

Pitfall 2

Pay attention to your self-talk while you're using this skill. Since this skill is typically used to avoid behaviors you might feel guilt, shame, or embarrassment about, it's easy to fall into shit-talking yourself through the process. This self-talk might look like saying, "I'm stupid for wanting to do this," "I'm crazy," and "It shouldn't be this difficult." Since most problem behaviors are triggered by high stress or big emotions in the first place, **shaming yourself is more likely to increase your risk of engaging in the behavior you're trying to avoid.** If possible, talk to yourself in the way you would speak to a child going through a difficult moment. Aim to be soothing, compassionate, and kind. If you're using ride the wave, you're already in a difficult moment. There's no reason to make it any harder for yourself.

Pitfall 3

Initial experiences of riding the wave can be beyond difficult. Kate has described her first experience of riding the wave as an absolute nightmare (it was worth it, but still one of the most unpleasant experiences of her life). For some, the second experience feels better, or it may feel just as hard. The third time can also be wildly unpredictable: you may start to notice getting the hang of it or feel like you're right back to the first time all over again. The takeaway here is that riding the wave isn't a linear process. **It is hard to predict when it will feel easier and when it will feel harder.** Try not to have expectations about what the experience will look like, and instead meet yourself where you are and allow the experience to unfold as it will.

BENEFITS

Benefit 1

So much of DBT is about not making a challenging situation worse, and ride the wave is no exception. With the previous example about a partner saying they want to talk, there were two different paths to go down: a "not-skillful" path (driving over to their house, drinking) or a "skillful path" (calling a friend, going for a walk). Imagine for a moment if the not-skillful path had been taken and if you had stayed home and gotten drunk. What then? Perhaps you would have drunk-dialed them or maybe you would have felt hungover going into work the next morning. No matter what, it likely wouldn't have made things any better. When you ride the wave, most of the time you're doing that because you don't have tools at your disposal to actually make the stressful situation better; you're just trying to not make it worse. **Ride the wave acts as prevention for impulsive choices that could have real consequences later.**

Benefit 2

Riding the wave is no small feat. Everything in you may so badly want to do the urge you've turned to many times before. Doing something the first time is often the hardest, and this is definitely true with riding the wave. If you've turned to a problem behavior 99 times before and now you're trying a new skillful behavior for the first time, it's going to feel extremely difficult to do. One thing we hear over and over again is that **people feel proud of themselves when they ride the wave**. Though that feeling of pride may come later (after the exhaustion phase has passed), you will likely look back on this and feel impressed that you had the willpower to get through it.

Benefit 3

Riding the wave tends to be a profound experience for many people, one that sometimes feels like a rite of passage or new beginning. It has the potential to set people on a new path the next time they encounter a strong action urge following an overwhelming event. **Riding the wave for any length of time matters and will help you build up to riding it for longer periods of time in the future.** Remember: growth is not linear. You may have ridden the wave once, and the next time done a problem behavior initially, but you are still setting yourself on a path for positive change every time you think about this concept and try it. Over time, it will become easier.

EXERCISE

Can you identify what action urge *you* have that ride the wave would be most helpful for?

What do you think is going to be the hardest part for you about ride the wave? The easiest?

Can you think of any times in your past when you wish you'd had this skill?

PART 4

INTERPERSONAL EFFECTIVENESS

Interpersonal effectiveness skills help with asking for what you want, fostering and repairing relationships, and saying no while maintaining your self-respect. These skills provide the framework for setting healthy boundaries and responding skillfully to others.

Chapter 19

DEAR MAN

ABOUT THIS SKILL

Articulating needs does not come naturally to most people. This can be due to growing up in a household where needs were suppressed and not spoken about. It can also come from being in a household where needs were voiced in a manipulative, passive-aggressive, or overtly antagonistic way. As an adult, you may struggle to avoid following in the footsteps of the adults you saw growing up.

Similarly to STOP, DEAR MAN is an acronym that is meant to be done in order for the "DEAR" portion. For the skill to be effective, each letter of "DEAR" must be done in the correct sequence. The "MAN" part talks about the kind of presence you want to have when doing the steps laid out in "DEAR."

The purpose of DEAR MAN is "objectives effectiveness," meaning you are making an attempt at "getting what you want" (Linehan 2015, p.125). DEAR MAN is the skill to turn to when asking someone for help or a favor, or to articulate relationship needs that are not being met. The focus is on getting your needs met, first and foremost. DEAR MAN provides a framework for how to ask for what you want from someone skillfully. Addressing each of the components in the skill will help you avoid common pitfalls most people experience when making requests. If you avoid these pitfalls, you're more likely to get a yes response from the other person. While this skill allows you to be more effective, because it involves other people it's possible to use the skill perfectly and still not get what you want. Nothing is guaranteed.

DEAR MAN can be used to say no to someone as well. Instead of asking for a request when doing the third step of "assert," you say no (in a single sentence). While DEAR MAN can certainly be used for saying no and setting a boundary, we believe the FAST skill is a better fit for that. For this reason, we will only talk about DEAR MAN in the context of making requests.

DESCRIBE (ONE TO TWO SENTENCES)

When making a request, it's necessary to give context for why you're asking this of the other person. In one to two sentences, explain what happened that led to you making this request in the first place. The key here is to be as objective as possible using neutral language (for example say, "You left the house last night" instead of saying "You stormed out last night"; say, "We were late to the appointment" instead of "You were running behind and made us late to the appointment"). If you and the other person can't agree on the circumstances surrounding the request, you may get stuck going back and forth about what happened and never getting to the part of asking for what you need. When the description of events is objective, it starts the request off on a note of commonality because you both know what you're talking about and can agree that what you're saying happened did take place.

EXPRESS (ONE TO TWO SENTENCES)

This is where you address any thoughts/emotions you have about the event you just described. This part is also kept to just one to two sentences. If you start to share more than that and find yourself telling the other person at length about how the event impacted you, you are no longer focusing on the request. The purpose of this step is to explain *why* you're making the request you're about to state. For example, you may be making this request because the situation you just talked about left you feeling worried or overwhelmed. You want the other person to know how you feel about the situation, so they have further insight into your perspective.

ASSERT (ONE SENTENCE)

Here it is! This is where you actually make your request. In a single sentence, state as specifically as you can what you would like from the other person. If you're talking to a boss about a raise, you could say, "I would like a 3 percent raise" instead of "I would like a raise"; if you're talking to your child about keeping their room clean, you could say, "I would like all of your clothes in your hamper before you go to bed each night" instead of "I would like you to keep your room cleaner." If your request is not specific enough, the person may misunderstand what you're looking for. It is recommended to phrase your request as a sentence rather than a question (for example, "I would like your help with this project" instead of "Can you help me with this project?"). This helps you appear confident with your request. You're also not done with your request yet (there's still the "R" in the next step!) and if you state your request as a question, the person may answer before you continue (and the next step is crucial in determining whether they agree to your request or not).

REINFORCE (ONE SENTENCE)

This final sentence is where you can state any positive benefits the other person may receive if they fulfill your request or how it may benefit the relationship between the two of you. It's important to put yourself in their shoes for a moment and think about what's in it for them. DBT states you can also "clarify the negative consequences of not getting what you want or need" (Linehan 2015, p.125), but we believe it's best to focus on the potential positive outcome for them whenever possible. For example, if you're asking a friend to help you with moving, you can tell them you'll return the favor. If you're asking someone to attend an event that's important to you, tell them the fun things happening at the event that you think will matter to them or how much it will mean to you to have them there. At first glance, this step can be perceived as bribery or manipulation in an attempt to get the person to say yes. In actuality, all this step does is explain what will happen if they do say yes; they don't *have* to say yes, but it's important for them to know that if they decide to do so, there's something good coming their way. Everything in life has a consequence, either positive or negative (going to work and doing your job leads to the positive consequence of a paycheck; if you don't show up to work, the negative consequence is you could be fired/have less income). This step also shows you're thinking about their needs and how this situation could potentially benefit them as well.

(STAY) MINDFUL

Remember: the purpose of DEAR MAN is to focus on getting *this* request met. The person you're talking to may have requests of their own they want to talk to you about or they may try to change the subject because they don't want to say yes to your request (and may not want to directly tell you no). Occasionally, the person may strongly dislike the request you're making and turn to personal attacks to tell you why they think you shouldn't be making this request. If any of these scenarios happen, you can try a couple different strategies to stay mindful:

If they bring up their own requests/past concerns or issues

Consider saying something like, "I am happy to talk about that with you some other time. Right now, I'd like us to stay focused on talking about ___." If they continue to bring up the same topic, you can say, "I already told you we can talk about that in a separate conversation if it's a concern for you. For now, we are talking about ___."

Personal attacks/defensiveness

Keep your voice tone/volume calm and steady, and continue to appear confident (next step). You can address this by saying things like, "It seems like this is hard for you to hear, but it is not okay for you to say ___ to me." You can also ask them to "listen and keep an open mind" as you're talking by saying something like, "I do want to hear your thoughts and concerns, but please let me finish first with what I would like to say." If they refuse to do that, it is in your best interest to end the conversation and come back to it later (be specific about when you want to talk about it again). You can do that by saying, "I want us to have this conversation when we are both in a better frame of mind. Let's come back to this tomorrow."

APPEAR CONFIDENT

You can say all the right words, but if your body language shows you're nervous about making your request, you're less likely to receive a yes answer. Speak at a volume that can easily be heard without being too loud. Make eye contact, and do your best to refrain from saying "um" too much as you're talking. If you're sitting while you make your request, sit up straight and try to keep your body still (no leg bouncing, fidgeting, etc.). If you're standing, make sure you're not crossing your arms, leaning against a wall, and so on. Practicing beforehand with a trusted other or looking in the mirror can help you get comfortable with what you're going to say. If the person initially says no, continue to appear confident as you move into the final step of negotiation.

NEGOTIATE

Ideally, after you've done the four steps of "DEAR" (while appearing confident throughout and staying mindful), the person says yes to your request. If this happens, there's no need to negotiate. But if you receive an initial no, it's time to negotiate. The "DEAR" part of this skill is typically quick, as you'll see with the scenarios that follow; the negotiation can sometimes take far longer, which makes it an important part of this skill. The word "negotiation" can have negative connotations, and many people believe they can't negotiate successfully. In fact, this part of the skill is all about turning the tables over to the other person; lessen your request to something that will still meet your needs and see if it will work for them. Perhaps you asked a friend to talk to you on the phone because you're having a hard day and they say they can't talk right then. Negotiating might look like asking them if they are available later in the day or if another day would work better for them. At the heart of negotiation is not taking a no answer as all-or-nothing. The person may only be saying no to part of your request. If you're asking your boss for a raise, they may say you can't have a raise now, but that you can have a raise in three months. If you ask a friend to go out to dinner with you, they may not be able to go out to dinner, but maybe they're able to go to coffee instead. Get curious about what will work for the other person and try to find a middle ground.

DEAR MAN IN ACTION

Let's look at this skill at work in two different scenarios. The components of the skill are labeled in parentheses.

Scenario 1: Asking roommate for help with household responsibilities

"This week I'm scheduled to work overtime at work (D). I'm really worried about being able to juggle what they're asking me to do and all the chores I know need to get done around here (E). I would like it if you're able to do the dishes every night this week (A). I'd be happy to return the favor for you in the future if you have a really busy week (R)."

Possible negotiations: "Would it work to do the dishes at least three times this week if every night is too much?" "Would you want to take on cooking dinner instead of dishes?" "What ideas do you have for helping out with chores this week that would feel do-able to you?"

Scenario 2: Asking romantic partner for increased communication
"The last three times I've texted you it's taken you more than eight hours to respond back to me (D). I understand life can get busy, but I also start to feel disconnected from you when I don't hear from you for long stretches of time (E). It would mean a lot to me if you're able to text me back within an hour of me texting you when you're not at work (A). I really think this would make our relationship better (R)."

Possible negotiations: "If texting back within an hour isn't realistic, would it work to text back within three hours?" "Would there be a better way for us to communicate besides texting?" "What feels realistic to you for how often we can make sure we're checking in with each other?"

POINTERS FOR SUCCESS WITH DEAR MAN
Here are a couple other things we have found to be helpful when using DEAR MAN.

When you make your request is important
If your request truly can't wait or you're not making a big request, it's likely that doing DEAR MAN at the first opportunity will be effective with most people, most of the time. Though there may not ever be a perfect time to make a big request, there are clearly circumstances and situations where doing so would be inappropriate and would decrease your chances of receiving a yes answer. If the other person is busy with another conversation, wait for the conversation to conclude instead of interrupting in the middle. If they've had a particularly stressful day, it may be best to wait until another day when they're back to baseline emotionally. We also advise against making big requests when someone is just about to leave or just returning home from work, and immediately in the morning or right before bed. This may leave you thinking there is no good time! In general, times that tend to be better are times between transitions, such as in between dinner and preparing for bed (if you want to talk with someone you live with like a child, partner, or roommate). Try to minimize distractions as much as you can. It may be helpful to schedule a meeting with a supervisor so both of you have set aside time in your calendars to talk. The same idea can apply with talking to a friend or someone else you don't live with; ask them if they have some time when they're free to talk and put it on the calendar.

You can ask a question after you've done all of the steps of "DEAR"

As mentioned previously, phrasing your request as a question during the "A" part of "DEAR" can result in the "R" never being addressed or appearing to not be confident in what you're asking for. However, it can be effective to ask a question after you've completed the four steps of "DEAR." You can then say something like, "How does that sound to you?" or "What do you think about that?" This makes it clear you have said what you wanted to say and that you would now like to turn it over to the other person to say yes or no to your request. After they give their answer, then you can begin negotiating (if needed).

KATE'S TIPS

I have traditionally had a terrible time when it comes to asking people for things I want or need. There has been more than one occasion where I cried my way through making a request with a boss. The anxiety is real! That said, I appreciate DEAR MAN more because of how much I struggle with requests. DEAR MAN hasn't cured my anxiety around asking for things, but it does give me a formula for making my request *despite* my anxiety. Here are a few things I do to make sure I have a firm hold of the skill when I need it in high anxiety situations.

Tip 1: Start incredibly small

The tactic here is to practice making small, inconsequential requests. Asking for a raise is *hard*. Negotiating chores with partners or housemates is *hard*. So many of the situations where we would practice DEAR MAN are inherently very stressful and sometimes can have far-reaching consequences. What a nerve-wracking space in which to be trying to learn a skill! While you want to progress past the little asks eventually, it's great to practice this skill about silly things when you're starting out (asking someone to pass you the salt, asking to go see the movie you want, asking for a small favor from a friend, etc.). The goal is simply to practice, practice, practice the skill. By practicing it in low-risk situations, you get the chance to drill the skill into your mind before you try it out "for real."

Tip 2: Start with safe people

Make sure you're being selective about your practice partner if you choose to practice this skill when you are starting out. Avoid people who stigmatize mental health issues, who have belittled or mocked you in the past, or people around whom you simply feel uncomfortable. Much like it is a lot to ask of yourself to try to learn DEAR MAN in difficult situations, it's a lot to ask of yourself to learn the skill with difficult people. Rather, you want to practice with people who you feel comfortable explaining the skill to and who will "play along" to help you get practice. In no time, you'll be an absolute pro at DEAR MAN, and you'll be ready to use it in more real-life situations.

Tip 3: Celebrate the attempts and not the victories

As humans, we are far more motivated to chase continued success than to try to continue past a failure. For this reason, it's important to keep an air of self-compassion around this skill. As you're learning and practicing DEAR MAN, chances are you will "fail" a lot. This might look like forgetting elements of the skill in the moment, getting pulled off track and not being able to remain mindful, not getting your request fulfilled, and so on. These may seem like failures at first blush, but they are actually victories because the victory is in the trying. Even if you forget parts, do parts incorrectly, or you don't get the result you want, you still *tried*. You tried to do things differently than you usually do. That's *hard*. And that's a *win*.

MICHELLE'S TIPS

DEAR MAN has been a tough skill for me to use over the years. As someone who chronically overthinks and worries about creating conflict, I hold back on making requests out of concern my request won't be "good enough" or that it will lead to a disagreement with the person I'm talking to if they say no to me or don't like my request in the first place. It has taken me a lot of work with my own therapist to become more confident asking for what I would like (and I'm still working at it!).

Tip 1: Their response to your request has nothing to do with you

There are many examples in life where two people experience the same event but have completely different responses to it. Let's say you go up to two co-workers at your job to ask for their help with a task. One of them happily says yes and the other refuses. Why did this happen? Their responses were likely influenced by how their day was going before your request was made and have nothing to do with how well or poorly you used DEAR MAN. So often in life when we receive a response we don't want, we think we are the sole reason for failure. In reality, a person's response to your request is influenced by a variety of factors including their personality, past experiences, current mood, and more. If your requests are consistently denied, you may want to review DEAR MAN again and make sure you're truly doing the skill correctly, but more often than not, it's not your fault if someone says no. Remember this when you feel disappointed in things not going as you hoped.

Tip 2: What is at the heart of your request?

Before you use DEAR MAN take some time to reflect and think about why you're making your request and what you're really hoping for. Perhaps you plan to ask your partner to start going out on dates with you once a week, and they say they don't think this is possible (because of money, limited time, etc.). As you move into negotiation, think about what you really want. Are you wanting more quality time with them (even if it's just at home)? Are you wanting to get out of the house more (whether it's with your partner or with a friend)? If you don't know what you're actually wanting, get clear on that before you ask. It will help guide you during negotiation to know what you're actually after.

Tip 3: Prepare without planning

For a long time, I rehearsed repeatedly what I was going to say. I had an "opening argument" planned out word for word. Once I worked up the courage to tell the person my concerns, they would respond...and I would promptly fall silent, not knowing what to say in the moment. When you create and memorize a DEAR MAN script, you're mostly just focusing on the "DEAR" which then leaves you woefully unprepared with the "MAN" components (and those three elements are so important!). I want you to have an idea of what you're going to say, and it's a good idea to practice it out loud a couple times; this preparation can really help. But know where to draw the line between feeling prepared and starting to plan out everything you'll say. There's no way to actually anticipate how the other person is going to respond, and they may sense that what you're saying is not happening spontaneously. Though you may have some mistakes along the way, trust the process after some initial preparation, and go with the flow in the moment with your responses.

PITFALLS

Pitfall 1

If your request is too vague, it's highly unlikely that you'll get what you're asking for. Asking for things like "I want to see you more" or "I need to feel loved" aren't specific enough. Misunderstandings are more likely with vague requests because the other person may think they are doing what you asked, while you believe they aren't. For best results, be as specific as possible. To fix those examples, you might say, "I'd like us to have at least one hour of dedicated time together every night" or "Would you please text me on your lunch break?" Both of those are specific, concrete requests, which means they are more likely to be both understood and followed.

Pitfall 2

Something that can be a struggle for some folks is remaining succinct with requests. **People can get way too detailed with describing the situation or with expressing how they feel about it before even getting to the request itself.** While this is an understandable inclination, it's one you have to fight in order to perform DEAR MAN effectively. A good rule is to keep both the D and the E to one sentence each. If you absolutely *must*, you can stretch it to two sentences. Talking more than that can muddy the waters and confuse the person you're speaking to. You want to be clear and concise so they easily keep track of and understand what you're saying. Writing out a DEAR MAN script ahead of time really helps with this. You can start by writing as much as you want, and then you can edit it down until the D and E are one or two sentences each.

Pitfall 3

We don't know about you, but we started out wildly anxious every time we tried to use DEAR MAN. Heck, we *still* get anxious at times about it! **Anxiety makes it hard to stay mindful and negotiate.** It's easy to get knocked off track or to just give up the moment someone pushes back or says no. Writing out your DEAR MAN script ahead of time (especially for negotiating) can help with knowing in advance what your bottom line is (no matter how scattered or anxious you are in the moment, you'll be more likely to stick to it). If you know the person well, you can think of responses to arguments they often pose (though be careful to avoid thinking you are a mind reader!). As for staying mindful, try simple, subtle grounding techniques during the conversation (such as wiggling your toes, willing hands, or noticing your surroundings). The more you practice mindfulness in other contexts, the easier it will be to use it when doing DEAR MAN.

BENEFITS

Benefit 1

DEAR MAN spells out step by step how to make a request. Many people like the structure this skill provides and how it covers all the bases. Without using DEAR MAN, people often overlook at least one component. Maybe they don't describe the situation before stating what they'd like, or they don't say what they're feeling emotionally. Staying mindful and appearing confident are important reminders about body language mattering and sticking to the topic at hand. We say in our DBT groups that you don't have to DEAR MAN *every* request. On the other hand, for bigger requests, people often don't know what to say and don't feel right just blurting out what they want. **DEAR MAN was created just for this reason so that you're able to talk about what you would like and why in an order that makes sense and checks all the boxes.**

Benefit 2

This may be mind blowing: you can ask for *anything* you want from *anybody* you want. That doesn't mean you're going to get a "yes" answer or that the other person will respond positively to your request, but there's nothing stopping you from asking except your own worries about their response. While your worries may be valid based on past history, this doesn't mean you should sweep what you want under the rug. Though we joke about the absurdity of using DEAR MAN for tiny requests, we also encourage people who struggle with making requests to practice this skill with silly situations like asking someone to pass the salt at dinner. This begins with identifying your needs, which then leads to the ask itself. **One thing we love about this skill is that it can be done with *any* request at all, big or small.** Once you overcome your worry about questioning if it's "okay" to make a request, just start trying.

Benefit 3

The negotiation piece of DEAR MAN helps bring the conversation to a close with what is hopefully a win for both people. Even though this is not always possible, as you're doing the other six components of the skill before negotiation, you can state what you'd like while also paying attention to the other person's experience of you making the request. Negotiation is not about "winning," and that's what is great about this part of the skill. **Negotiation brings in dialectical thinking, and when you are thinking dialectically it becomes easier for you to put yourself in the other person's shoes.** You don't have to alter the heart of your request, but you can work on finding something that will work for you both or establishing a middle ground.

EXERCISE

Is there one part of DEAR MAN that you think you already do well? Can you give an example?

Which of the components of DEAR MAN are you the most worried to try? Why?

Do you think you will end up using DEAR MAN more in your personal life or your professional life? Why?

Chapter 20

GIVE

ABOUT THIS SKILL

The key to keeping relationships healthy in the long run is to communicate with empathy and understanding for the other person's perspective. When you show the person you're talking to that you care about them and what they have to say, the relationship grows stronger. Unfortunately, relationships are often riddled with misunderstandings, disagreements, and hurt feelings. One or both people get caught up in wanting to be "right" and lose sight of nourishing the relationship. When the relationship starts to suffer in this way, GIVE is the skill to turn to.

The purpose of GIVE is to improve and nourish your relationship with another person. When using GIVE, you focus all of your attention on what the other person is sharing with you, showing them kindness and interest as you listen. Communicating this way at all times with other people can lead to you disregarding your own needs and avoiding addressing concerns you may have, so it's important to be intentional about when to use this skill. GIVE can be used for a wide range of reasons at all stages of a relationship. When a relationship is new and just forming, GIVE can help the relationship get off the ground. The person you're getting to know will likely appreciate the interest and validation they feel from you and want to spend more time with you. When a relationship inevitably hits a bump in the road, using the elements of GIVE when apologizing can help the relationship get back on track and repair hurts. When a relationship starts to feel stagnant over time, conversations using GIVE can help both people feel more connected to one another again. We also think GIVE is the perfect go-to skill when interacting with someone who is grieving or going through a hard time.

Unlike the DEAR in DEAR MAN, the four components of GIVE are not done in order; instead, they are all done at once as you interact with the other person.

(BE) GENTLE

When someone is being gentle with us, we often will physiologically feel calmer in our bodies. The word gentle may seem synonymous with words like meek, quiet, or shy, but it really means being understanding, patient, and kind. Being gentle shows the other person the conversation they are engaged in is a safe conversation, one in which they have the space to be open and which allows room for them to express themselves. Being gentle may look like slowing down the pace of conversation to give the other person space. Being gentle may also look like using physical touch to convey concern or to create closeness. Some phrases that imply gentleness are "I'm here for you," "I want to understand your point of view," or "Take all the time you need." If being gentle feels unnatural to you, you can say to the other person, "Can you tell me what I can do that would help you feel comfortable in this conversation?" Whatever you do after that will likely be gentle.

(ACT) INTERESTED

This part of GIVE is all about body language. Most communication is not actually about the words you say and is instead about what is not being said in words (your posture, tone of voice, how close you stand to someone, etc.; Mehrabian 1972). Your body language says it all about how interested you are in the other person. If you're looking at your phone, looking away, yawning, or have a closed body posture, your actions make it clear you're not interested. Even though the "I" in GIVE stands for Interested, the "act" that comes before it is important. There will be times when you do not have interest in what someone is sharing with you. Perhaps you're tired, or they're talking about a topic you don't care about or is confusing to you. Without meaning to, your body language may convey a lack of interest, and this damages the relationship, often leaving the other person feeling hurt and alone. At first glance, "acting" interested may appear disingenuous or as if you're lying. In fact, it is an intentional choice that shows you care and don't want to hurt their feelings. While we certainly don't expect you to act interested *all* the time with what *anyone* is sharing, try to notice those particular times when someone you care about is excited about something, for example, and see if you can be there for them in the way they'd like you to be.

VALIDATE

This is the most important part of GIVE. The entire purpose of the skill is to show the other person you're there for them. You want to show them you understand their side of a disagreement, that you support them in their interests or goals, and that they can lean on you during hard times. Sometimes validating another person feels nearly impossible if you have two very different opinions about a topic. Validation is not about saying you think they're right when you disagree. Validation is about saying you see the reasons for their opinion based on who they are, their life experience, and so on. It's not about changing your view to theirs or going against your morals/values for the sake of another person. If your first instinct is to disagree and talk about all the reasons why your position is better, this isn't validating their perspective. Instead, this turns into you talking about yourself and putting the spotlight on you. Validation can look many different ways and can include saying things like, "I can see why you did that," "That is so hard to be going through," "I would feel scared, too," and "It seems like you're really trying to make this work."

(USE AN) EASY MANNER

In other words, add some lightness and humor (only if appropriate!) to the situation. Why is this important for helping others feel validated? Because it shows you're human! Just focus on being yourself and supporting the other person with an open mind and by being genuine. Make sure you're not censoring yourself *too* much in an effort to make a good impression on someone new. You want the other person to get a taste of who you really are so they can decide if they want to get to know you more.

GIVE IN ACTION

Below are two different scenarios when using GIVE would be appropriate. After each scenario are examples of validating comments and invalidating comments. The validating comments emphasize the principles of GIVE, and the invalidating comments demonstrate what to avoid saying.

Scenario 1: Offering support

You notice a co-worker at your job appears to be crying. You approach them to ask what's wrong and they tell you they're feeling overwhelmed trying to balance working overtime and their kids' extracurricular activities.

Validating comments: "That's a lot on your plate right now. No wonder you're feeling so overwhelmed." "It's really hard trying to do it all. No one can do it perfectly." "I can tell how much your kids mean to you and how it breaks your heart to not be able to be there."

Invalidating comments: "It's not that bad, you'll be back to your normal schedule soon without overtime." "I know someone who was missing out on their kids' activities too, but their kids understood so your kids will be fine, don't be so hard on yourself." "You just need to tell the boss you can't work overtime anymore and put your foot down."

Scenario 2: Building a new relationship

You're at a party for a friend and you don't know anyone. You approach someone who also appears to be alone and introduce yourself. As the two of you start talking, they begin telling you about a hobby of theirs you know nothing about.

Validating comments: "Wow, I can tell how much you love this!" "That must be really cool to get to spend so much time on your passion." "Tell me more about how you got into this."

Invalidating comments: "I have no clue what you're talking about." "That's not my cup of tea." "What I really enjoy doing is..." (change the subject to talk about your hobby).

KATE'S TIPS

This is my favorite of the interpersonal skills. GIVE is not only well suited to my nature, but it is also well aligned with my professional presence as a therapist. However, GIVE coming easily to me can sometimes be a problem because I stop paying attention to the skill. Once you think you know something inside and out, the temptation is to do it on autopilot. On autopilot, I'm much more likely to look disinterested (looking at my phone, for example), give unsolicited advice, or overshare and steal the spotlight. I might, if I'm trying to repair a relationship, accidentally start becoming defensive. There are all kinds of ways I might deviate from doing GIVE well if I just coast and stop paying attention. I'll relate to you some ways I work to stay on track with this skill.

Tip 1: Make sure GIVE is the right tool for the job

It's always best to start by confirming that GIVE is the correct skill for the goal I'm trying to accomplish. In most interpersonal interactions, the relationship with the other person involved is of at least *some* importance to you. I think it is because of this that it can (at least for me) be difficult at times to know if GIVE is the skill you want to be reaching for. Since you're probably trying to tend to the relationship with the other person to one degree or another, the best idea here is to look for what your *primary* goal is in the situation. Are you actually trying first and foremost to set a boundary? Get a need met? If your top priority isn't trying to build, nurture, or repair a relationship, then GIVE is not the skill to use.

Tip 2: Get into a state of mindfulness before you head into the interaction

Being mindful helps to make sure you're present and that you don't slip into autopilot. You might try taking a few slow, deep breaths to ground yourself, practice half-smile or willing hands, or engage in almost any mindfulness activity you enjoy just to make sure you are in a present and aware state before entering the interaction. This is far more likely to set you up for successfully practicing GIVE once you're in the moment. If you struggle with staying present *during* interactions as well, I highly suggest noticing your feet; this can be a wonderful grounding exercise. You can wiggle your toes, flex your foot, or just notice your feet resting on the floor. Most of the time, if you can bring your awareness to your feet, you're going to be more present in the space around you as well.

Tip 3: Do a mental rundown of the letters in GIVE

As a sort of pre-flight checklist, it can be a good idea to consciously do a mental rundown of what each of the letters stands for in GIVE. If you have the time and space, you might even consider thinking about what elements of GIVE are usually the most difficult for you to practice well, and strategize around how to support yourself in performing them well in this situation. If the situation you're headed into is especially difficult for you, I would also suggest using cope ahead to imagine yourself using the skill correctly. Being mentally prepared and having already "seen" yourself using the skill correctly can do wonders for performing the skill well in the moment.

MICHELLE'S TIPS

When we teach GIVE in groups, most participants tend to think it's an easy skill. They tell us they're good listeners and always putting other people's needs first; they think they're experts at prioritizing and caring for their relationships. However, when we have them break out into pairs and practice GIVE, we find most people aren't actually doing GIVE. While they have good intentions, they commonly fall into some of the pitfalls we'll talk about next. Especially as a therapist, I like to think using GIVE is something that comes naturally to me, but I make mistakes too (especially when I'm not working with clients). Here are some of the mistakes I've made along with suggestions I hope will help you.

Tip 1: Think about the platinum rule

The golden rule states "Do unto others as you would have them do unto you." In other words, think about how you want to be treated and treat other people that same way. In recent years, the golden rule has gotten an upgrade to the "platinum rule." The platinum rule says to treat other people how *they* want to be treated instead of treating them how you would want someone to treat you (Alessandra and O'Connor 1996). What may work well for you may be a disaster for someone else. If you're not trying to understand their point of view, you're going to miss the boat with GIVE, even if you're saying some really nice, validating comments and have gentle, interested body language. Think about what the other person needs and how they would like you to be with them. If you don't know the person well this will be harder, but there's a simple thing you can do: just ask. Ask the person, "How can I best support you?" or "What would you like from me at this moment?" and make every effort to give it to them. Asking is in line with the platinum rule because it shows you don't want to make assumptions about what you think they may want.

Tip 2: Less is more

I'm a talker. I value communication highly, and when someone is having a hard time or if I need to apologize, I will talk much more than needed in an effort to be supportive and convey understanding. One thing I really like about GIVE is that you can practice three out of the four letters without saying a word (being gentle, acting interested, and using an easy manner). If you don't know what to say to someone, *don't say anything*. It's better to be silent with body language that communicates care than to keep talking when the other person may have a hard time taking in what you're saying. They say "actions speak louder than words" and it's true. Notice if you're starting to talk more than the other person, and acknowledge it in a way that feels comfortable to you (for example, "I've been talking a lot just now, I want to turn it back over to you so I can listen"). Lean on your facial expressions to communicate your emotions and what you're feeling rather than your words. Above all, start to notice if all that talking is inadvertently making it about you. Even if you're talking about the other person and their experience, to practice GIVE all the way you are going to be the follower in the conversation, and you'll need to let the other person lead as they speak.

Tip 3: Don't practice GIVE if you don't have anything to give

I have a hard time saying no to people. What this resulted in for many years was me making every effort to be there for the people I loved at all costs. Even if my emotional gas tank was running on empty, I would push myself to show up in the way others wanted me to. What I learned over many years of doing this is I really struggle to be gentle and act interested with other people when I'm emotionally depleted. I still have the ability to say the right things, but I have a hard time delivering my words gently, and acting interested feels like a huge chore. If you've had a long day, don't use GIVE until you've had a chance to take care of yourself and recharge your batteries. If someone wants a listening ear, tell them you want to listen when you're able to give your full attention (for example, "I want to be here for you and I don't think I can be at my best tonight after the day I've had. Does it work for us to talk tomorrow instead?"). This is the best way to prioritize the relationship, avoid potential emotional damage to the other person, and avoid burnout for yourself.

PITFALLS
Pitfall 1

When someone is sharing their woes with you, it's natural to think of experiences you've had that are similar. In normal, everyday conversation we often pipe up and talk about our own experience, usually with the hope of conveying understanding and empathy for what the other person is going through. While you may be able to mention a similar experience in passing without stepping outside the bounds of GIVE, it is usually best avoided. **The risk is that you may inadvertently take over the conversation, making yourself the focus instead of your conversation partner.** Even if that isn't your intention, it can still happen. If you want to convey a similar feeling without that risk, you can make more generalized statements. For instance, instead of saying, "You know, I lost my dad too, so I know how hard that is," you might try "Grief can be so hard, I'm sorry you're going through this right now."

Pitfall 2

When you care about someone, or you are trying to foster or nurture a relationship with someone new, it makes sense to want to provide them with help, support, and guidance (especially if that person is expressing some hardship or struggle). **While there are absolutely appropriate times and spaces to offer advice or problem solving to those around you, GIVE is not about finding solutions to other people's problems.** Unless the person you're in conversation with explicitly asks you to give your opinion or advice, do your best to avoid it. You can simply say something like, "Let me know if there's anything I can do to help support you here." That lets them know that you are open to being a resource, without pushing them to take unwanted advice.

Pitfall 3

People sometimes think GIVE equates to becoming a doormat. This isn't true at all! The purpose of GIVE is to foster, nurture, or repair a relationship. While you can adopt some of the mannerisms described in GIVE in other circumstances, it is not the skill to use if you are asking for something, saying no, or setting a boundary. Being gentle, interested, validating, and having an easy manner doesn't mean saying yes to everything requested of you or allowing someone to treat you poorly (those are times to use FAST instead of GIVE). Switch between skills to one more appropriate if the purpose of the interaction changes.

BENEFITS
Benefit 1

All relationships will experience conflict at some point if they continue for any length of time. **Arguably the biggest benefit of GIVE is that this skill helps repair ruptures when they occur and helps prevents ruptures in the first place.** If you're practicing GIVE consistently in your relationships, it's the equivalent of watering a plant. When you sense a relationship in your life needs some care and nurturing, practice GIVE in the next conversation you have with that person and notice what happens. If you have a relationship where the two of you struggle to make amends and move forward after a disagreement, give them some validation the next time you argue, and you'll likely have a different experience. The relationships that flourish in the long run are those where both people are doing GIVE on a regular basis with each other.

Benefit 2

Practicing GIVE well means being fully present and tuned in to what the other person is sharing. Even people who are very good listeners often focus on the past or the future. This becomes apparent if they start telling a story about themselves or someone else who experienced something similar (the past) or if they start giving advice about what they believe you should do next (the future). Taking the focus off the person who is sharing in these ways is the opposite of GIVE! To meaningfully validate someone requires full attunement to all of what they are saying and *not saying*. Notice their body language and tone of voice while listening to their words and the larger meaning behind them. If you struggle with being in the "now," **GIVE provides you with the tools you need to show up in conversations with others without your mind being elsewhere**. The person you're communicating with will be able to sense how engaged you are, and you'll likely find yourself less stressed in the conversation when you're being mindful and validating instead of trying to problem solve for the other person.

Benefit 3

Forming friendships in adulthood is not easy. It's hard to make the time to meet new people, have conversations that leave a good impression, and then invest time and energy into getting to know each other. **Using GIVE increases your chances of leaving a good impression on those you meet, hopefully leading to them wanting to get to know you more.** Out of all the people you know, think about the person who most uses GIVE with you. Chances are that time with this person feels distinctly different from others. Becoming that person for other people leads to you standing out in the best of ways. Not only can this help with forming friendships, but it also helps with dating relationships. If you struggle with coming up with topics to talk about or don't feel comfortable sharing much personally about yourself, GIVE makes it easier to follow the flow of conversation and keeps the focus on validating the other person's experience. If you notice you have a tendency to inadvertently keep the topic of conversation about yourself, practicing GIVE will help you make a shift to listening while others share.

EXERCISE

Do the elements of GIVE feel likely to come easily or naturally for you? Why or why not?

If there's one part of GIVE where you think you're the most likely to slip into autopilot, which is it, and why?

What's one relationship in your life right now where you'd like to employ GIVE and how do you think it would positively impact this relationship to use it?

Chapter 21

FAST

ABOUT THIS SKILL

Unfortunately, there will be times in relationships when someone wants you to do something that doesn't feel comfortable to you. FAST consists of four principles to guide you in turning down requests from others and standing up for your values. If you have historically struggled with setting boundaries or confidently telling people no, FAST is here to help you assert yourself and maintain your self-respect.

Because FAST is all about self-respect, this skill is used in situations where you want to prioritize your needs. One way you may know you need to use FAST is if you start to experience that uncomfortable pit in your stomach or lump in your throat when interacting with someone. Those are signs from your body that something about this interaction feels violating. The other person may be asking you to do something you don't want to do or attempting to engage you in a conversation you don't want to have because the topic is not one you feel comfortable discussing. If any boundary is being crossed for you, whether it's a physical boundary or an emotional boundary, use FAST to clearly and firmly tell the other person to stop. FAST can be used anytime you recognize the need to prioritize yourself.

Similar to GIVE, the four components of FAST are not done in order; they are all done at once as you respond to the other person.

(BE) FAIR

Though you are setting a boundary with the person you're interacting with, it's important to ensure you're doing this in a way that respects yourself and is respectful to them, too. Do not resort to raising your voice, name-calling, swearing at them, and so on. Speak to them calmly, and listen when they are speaking. Model respect for them the same way you are hoping for them to respect you. Beyond just being fair with your body language, consider adding in a validating phrase to show the other person you understand their perspective, while still asserting your boundary. If they make statements that are factually true or that you agree with, you can say something like, "You're right that I have said yes to this in the past, but this time I am deciding to make a different choice" or "I would feel the same way if I were in your shoes; however, I am still not able to help you in the way you'd like me to."

You can also tell them what you will do if you don't want to fulfill a request exactly as it's being asked as one method of practicing fairness. For example, you can say, "I won't be able to help you move all day, but I can help for two hours" or "I'm happy to loan you that book, but after a week I'd like to have it back."

(NO) APOLOGIES

This part of FAST may be the easiest to understand (simply refrain from saying "I'm sorry"), but it is one of the hardest parts to do when you're using the skill in real time. There are many reasons to apologize in life; after all, mistakes happen, and you may genuinely regret past things you've said and done. However, using FAST is not one of those times. Why? Because sticking to your values and respecting yourself is not a bad or wrong thing to do. Just because the other person doesn't like your decision, it does not mean you have to apologize to them. Oftentimes we apologize because we don't want the other person to get upset with us for telling them no, and we hope an apology will take the tension out of a situation. Not only does it often not serve that purpose (the tension may remain), but it can confuse the other person and lead them to believe you're not serious about holding your ground if you're "sorry" for the choice you're making. As you're doing the other components of FAST, make sure the words "I'm sorry" are not said. You may be surprised at how often you apologize without even thinking about it. This is an opportunity to start changing that.

STICK TO VALUES

This is at the heart of FAST and the piece of the skill that drives everything you say. A value is anything that is important to you. When you are saying no to someone, you're saying no for a reason. It's important to know what that reason is and to believe your reason matters. Some of the most common values that come up when practicing FAST are about taking care of oneself, time boundaries, and holding on to what is yours when someone else wants something you have (whether that be a physical object or emotional energy). If you don't hold on to your values, this can lead to poor self-care and deep unhappiness in the long run. There can be a misconception that sticking to your values is selfish or disregards the other person's needs. To the contrary, sticking to your values may actually lead to you helping other people more if lending a helping hand is an important value to you. Two people might have completely different responses while using FAST if they hold different values from each other. Once you are clear on what matters to you and you feel confident stating it, the other components of FAST fall into place more easily.

(BE) **T**RUTHFUL

It is an all-too-common experience to "make up an excuse" for why you're telling someone no. An example of this could be saying, "I have other plans already" when you're invited to an event you don't want to attend (even if you don't have anything scheduled on your calendar). So often we worry that being truthful will hurt someone's feelings, and so we try to soften the blow of saying no by giving a socially acceptable reason. If you keep the focus on your values, you already have your reason for saying no. For example, if you're invited to an event you don't want to attend, you could say, "I won't be attending because I prefer to go home and relax after work instead of going out with people" or "That sounds like it would be really fun, but I'm going to have a quiet night in that evening so I won't make it." In many cases, you may struggle to be truthful because you fear other people will challenge your reasons. This may happen at times, and if it does, you can practice repeating what you already said and reiterating your value.

FAST IN ACTION

Below are two different scenarios when you could use FAST to assert yourself. After each scenario is an example of using FAST in response. The components of the skill are labeled in parentheses.

Scenario 1: Saying no to loaning money

A friend is asking you to loan them money because they're not able to pay their rent this month. Even though you have the funds on hand to give them, you do not feel comfortable doing so.

You: No, I won't loan you that money (A).

Friend: Why not?

You: Loaning money to other people is something I don't feel comfortable doing (S, T). I've done it with other people in the past and not been paid back. I'm happy to help you in other ways, like if you need a ride somewhere (F).

Friend: You can trust me though, I've never broken a promise to you.

You: It's true you have kept your word in the past (F). This is just something I don't do for anyone (S).

Scenario 2: Saying no to working overtime

Your boss is asking you to work overtime. You have made the decision you won't work overtime on the weekends because you don't want to miss out on time with your family.

You: No, I can't work overtime tonight (A).

Boss: I really need you though, I don't have anyone else who can do it.

You: I understand you're in a bind (F), but I also have to make sure I'm taking care of myself outside of work (S). If you need me to work extra next week on a weekday, that may work, but not tonight (F).

Boss: Okay, but I may also need help next Saturday. Can you come in a little early next Saturday?

You: No, I won't work overtime on the weekends since that's my time with my kids (S, T). Helping out next week on a weekday is what I can do (F).

KATE'S TIPS

FAST is one of the most difficult DBT skills for me to practice. While I'm good at being fair to others, I struggle to be fair to myself. I'm prone to endless, unnecessary apologizing. Standing up for myself and sticking to my values can be difficult if conflict is intense. In order to avoid as much conflict as possible, I can easily find myself lying when saying no or setting a boundary. This skill is hard!

Tip 1: Access your wise mind

As I said, I'm prone to discounting my own wants, needs, emotions, desires, or limitations. I might expect things from myself I would never expect of others, or think my reasons for not wanting to do something aren't "good enough" for me to say no. If I can access my wise mind, chances are I can bring my reason mind more into the forefront to balance out the fears and guilt of my emotion mind. This helps me see I'm just as important and worthy as the person I'm interacting with and helps me with being more fair to myself.

Tip 2: Imagine a friend saying it

One of the things that gets in the way of me doing FAST is a misplaced sense of guilt, as I mentioned in the last tip. One way to tackle that is with my wise mind, but if I'm finding it hard to access my wise mind, I imagine a friend doing or saying the thing I'm struggling to do or say. If I would be understanding and supportive of them in that situation, it helps me understand and support myself better. If I wouldn't judge someone else as a bad, selfish, unkind person for the exact thing that I'm considering, then I can stand my ground a lot more firmly and with a lot less emotional baggage. If you're finding that you struggle mostly with judging yourself as a barrier to this skill, this tip may be your best starting point.

Tip 3: Choose your timing

Struggling to stick to my values is rooted in my childhood. I get easily triggered in conflict and end up dissociating, losing touch with my sense of self or my values. If I try to use FAST when I'm somewhere above a 7 on a 1 to 10 scale emotionally, it's simply not going to be successful. I'll be firmly in my emotion mind and unable to practice the skill mindfully. If you want to set yourself up for success with this skill, do your best to be in a decent emotional space. I understand you may not always get to choose when someone is going to ask you for something you don't want to give. However, you can be aware of how their request impacts you emotionally, and choose your skill from there. If the request sends you into an intense emotional state, don't jump right into FAST! Try walking away (maybe practicing STOP to take the time to get re-grounded) before trying to use FAST.

MICHELLE'S TIPS

For me, practicing FAST is extremely challenging. If you grew up in a family like mine, saying no to other people was frowned upon. I was expected to show up to events whether I wanted to or not and help people out when they asked because if I didn't do those things, it meant other people might potentially get upset. I got very good at doing the socially acceptable thing at the cost of violating what was important to me. Thankfully, due to years of therapy, I've gotten much better at practicing FAST (though I still slip up and apologize every once in a while!).

Tip 1: Learn from other people

Though FAST is a challenging skill for me, I know a few people in my life who find it easy to communicate in this way. I've tried to watch and learn from them when I see them sticking to their values without apologizing. I also find it helpful to be surrounded by others who are working on boundaries, just like I am. We support each other's triumphs and share empathy when we fall back into old habits. My hope for you is that you have at least one person in your life who is comfortable with asserting themselves. Let this person serve as inspiration for you. You're not going to do it exactly like them because you'll have your own style of boundary-setting, but they can at least serve as a reminder that it is possible to stand up for yourself.

Tip 2: Know your value and let that guide you

I believe that if you don't know what value you're sticking to FAST won't work. It will be all too easy to find yourself apologizing and potentially doing what is being asked of you, even if you don't want to. Before you even open your mouth to speak and try the skill, know why you're saying no. With the prior scenario of the employee who is refusing to work overtime, they know their reason why (they want time with their family). If the answer is just "I don't want to work," the person you're communicating with will likely sense you don't have a clear reason for why you're refusing. It doesn't really matter what the reason is. Maybe that employee was feeling tired and like they needed to go home and sleep instead of work later than anticipated; that honors the value of rest and prioritizing sleep. It could have been that on principle they refuse to work more than 40 hours a week; this respects the value of balancing life and work. Your value can be anything! All that matters is that you're clear on what it is and the purpose for setting your boundary. That is what you're ultimately communicating about the whole time.

Tip 3: Tell them what you *will* do

As suggested previously as a strategy to practice fairness, I am a huge fan of telling people "no to this, yes to that." This is a parenting technique that works well with children (and with adults!) that I learned when I was teaching parenting classes. This would be like a parent saying, "We can't go to the park, but we can go play in the backyard." When you use this approach, you're communicating that you want to find a compromise/solution that works for both people. Ending with the thing you're saying yes to also has the effect of people hearing your "yes" answer more prominently than the "no" answer you're giving initially. People don't like receiving no answers, so giving any kind of yes answer can take you far. For me, this feels much easier and more in alignment with who I am to make suggestions like this and attempt to find a middle ground.

PITFALLS
Pitfall 1

The first and possibly most common struggle with FAST is not apologizing. We have been teaching this skill for years, and we *still* occasionally apologize when we're doing example roleplays in groups! Have a lot of compassion for yourself when you mess this one up. The best advice for not accidentally having apologies slip out is to slow down. It is easy to start speaking quickly and rush through a situation that makes you uncomfortable. But the faster you are running through the conversation, the easier it is to lose track of what is about to come out of your mouth. Take a breath, speak slowly, and you're much more likely to notice *before* you apologize.

Pitfall 2

It can be *very* tempting to lie when saying no or setting a boundary. Many folks in groups through the years have struggled with the "stay truthful" aspect of FAST. So, if you're one of those people, what can you do? If at all possible, spend some time thinking about the conversation before you have it. Consider the thing you are saying no to, or the boundary you are setting. Does it really mean you are a bad person? Is it actually a hurtful thing to do? Guilt can become like a reflex, and so taking time to examine the situation and take a wise-mind view often helps reduce the guilt or anxiety you may be feeling. If you don't have the opportunity to plan ahead for the conversation, then the advice is the same for the first pitfall: slow down. Consider what you are going to say, and check in with your wise mind about whether lying is actually the best choice at that moment.

Pitfall 3

Finally, like many other DBT skills, it is so important to make sure FAST is the right skill for the situation you are in/problem you are trying to solve. While GIVE is used to help foster, nurture, or repair relationships, FAST is all about creating boundaries, saying no, and holding on to your self-respect. Another way you might conceive of it is to think that GIVE is for taking care of the other person, and FAST is all about taking care of yourself. In some situations, you may want to set a boundary while also wanting to prioritize the relationship at the same time. In situations like this, **you'll notice something feeling "off" when practicing FAST because your boundary is not what's most important to you**; the relationship with the other person matters more. If you aren't clear on what you're prioritizing, the skill won't work as effectively.

BENEFITS
Benefit 1

For those who struggle with FAST, the challenge of using this skill is typically rooted in a belief that saying no will hurt other people. Therefore, they rarely say no because they don't want to "hurt" someone. This leads to self-sacrifice and following along with what's expected of you, which negatively impacts your own mental health. Even if you are giving an answer or setting a boundary someone does not like, it is up to them to determine what they will do next (not up to you to solve their problem for them). **When you practice FAST, you are no longer carrying around other people's problems, requests, and worries.** You'll separate out what you can and will do and what doesn't work for you in a new way. FAST is the opposite of people-pleasing, and though it takes practice to communicate like this, you'll feel lighter once you feel comfortable with it.

Benefit 2

When it comes to communication, it takes two to tango. You don't have a magic wand to change how others communicate, but when you change yourself, the "dance" of communication will inevitably change with the other person. There may be plenty of people in your life who don't know how to react once you start using FAST, but hopefully there will be other people who appreciate and admire your use of this skill. If they also struggle with boundary-setting, they may feel inspired by your use of FAST. Once you start communicating with more fairness and truthfulness, this often leads to others following suit. The reason for that? It's refreshing to be honest. It's not easy to tell the truth at times, but then there are no games being played with communication (and that feels good!). **The more transparent you are, the more you may see vulnerability and honesty from others, too.**

Benefit 3

Living life according to your values and what matters to you is a powerful thing. If you've found yourself living a life of trying to please other people or simply doing what's expected of you on autopilot, you likely feel weighed down, anxious, or unhappy much of the time. Intentionally practicing FAST can set you free. Not every interaction is going to need FAST (in fact, you won't need this skill for most interactions), but if you start to notice something feeling out of alignment for you and you communicate that, **you're taking a crucial first step to re-claiming your well-being and what matters to you.** You can't be all things to all people; that's a recipe for burnout and overwhelm. If you don't know where to start, you can begin by picking one value you've lost sight of and noticing what you want to do differently to get back in touch with that value. Then all you have to do is communicate what you're doing to other people as needed, and before you know it, you're doing FAST and living more authentically.

EXERCISE

Is there a part of FAST where you already feel like you really know what you're doing? If so, which part?

FAST can be intimidating to a lot of people. Is there a part that intimidates you?

Can you think of any recent examples of times you could have used FAST?

Chapter 22

IN CONCLUSION

If reading this book was your first introduction to DBT, and you think you'd like to dive further into the skills, there are a number of ways you can make that happen. We agree that the best way to learn and integrate DBT skills fully is by participating in DBT skills groups while also seeing a DBT therapist. However, for various and sundry reasons, that may not be the right (or accessible) path for you. If you have to pick one of the two, we tend to believe that DBT is best delivered in a group setting, due to getting to hear the questions and experiences of others in the group with you. On the other hand, some may choose to only see an individual DBT therapist. This is great for folks who really want or need to work through material at their own pace or are simply too uncomfortable to learn well in a group environment. And if you either are unable to access those resources, or if you just don't feel as though you are looking to dive *that* deep into DBT, there are lots of online community spaces where you can find others to talk to about skills and get support around utilizing DBT in your day-to-day life.

Speaking of utilizing DBT in your day-to-day life, the best way to make the most of these skills can be summarized in two words: go slowly. Give yourself time to practice these skills. Anything new that you try is going to take time and repetition before it becomes comfortable, let alone instinctual. And the more distressed you feel, the harder new skills become to remember; this is why patience and practice are key. Whether you came to this book as a refresher or if this is your first pass at these skills, it still makes sense to take your time. Focus on one skill (or *maybe* two) for a week, two weeks, or even longer. Find new and different ways to interact with the skill. You could journal, teach the skill to a friend or a child, or make art inspired by the skill. Just stick with it and keep rehearsing it until it becomes something akin to second nature to reach for the skill when it would be appropriate. It's *then* that you move to the next skill on which you want to focus.

So, that's where to find the skills and how to bring them into your life, but what is at the heart of this book? When we first began writing, we already knew what we hoped our readers would take away at the end. First and foremost, we wish for you to take away *something* that is useful to you, whether that be at least one skill you are excited to try or a skill you've tried while reading and are excited to continue to practice. We also fervently hope that you come away knowing that DBT is for everyone. No matter your mental health diagnosis, or lack thereof, there is something here for everyone. Everyone struggles, and no one has all the answers for how to handle struggling with grace. That in turn leads into our final ambition, which is that you finish this book and walk away feeling validated. We want each and every one of you reading this book to see yourself reflected somewhere in these pages, and we want you to know that your struggles and hardships are valid. Everyone needs support and everyone needs skills.

References

Alessandra, T. and O'Connor, M.J. (1996) *The Platinum Rule*. New York: Hachette Book Group.

Anderson, E. and Shivakumar, G. (2013) 'Effects of exercise and physical activity on anxiety.' *Front Psychiatry* 4, 27.

Barnes, A. (2020) *The 4 Day Week: How the Flexible Work Revolution Can Increase Productivity, Profitability and Wellbeing, and Help Create a Sustainable Future*. London: Hachette UK.

Blankert, T. and Hamstra, M.R.W. (2017) 'Imagining success: Multiple achievement goals and the effectiveness of imagery.' *Basic and Applied Social Psychology* 39, 1, 60–67.

Burton, R.A. (2019) Our Brains Tell Stories So We Can Live. Nautilus. Accessed on 07/03/23 at https://nautil.us/our-brains-tell-stories-so-we-can-live-237501/

Bushman, B.J., Dewall, C.N., Pond Jr., R.S. and Hanus, M.D. (2014) 'Low glucose related to greater aggression in married couples.' *Proceedings of the National Academy of Sciences of the United States of America* 111, 17, 6254–6257.

Carey, B. (2011) 'Expert on mental illness reveals her own fight.' *New York Times*, June 23, 2011.

Cay, M., Ucar, C., Senol, D., Cevirgen, F. *et al.* (2018) 'Effect of increase in cortisol level due to stress in healthy young individuals on dynamic and static balance scores.' *Northern Clinics of Istanbul* 5, 4, 295–301.

Chawla, N., MacGowan, R.L., Gabriel, A.S. and Podsakoff, N.P. (2020) 'Unplugging or staying connected? Examining the nature, antecedents, and consequences of profiles of daily recovery experiences.' *Journal of Applied Psychology* 105, 1, 19–39.

Coffeng, J.K., van Sluijs, E.M., Hendriksen, I.J.M., van Mechelen, W. and Boot, C.R. (2015) 'Physical activity and relaxation during and after work are independently associated with the need for recovery.' *Journal of Physical Activity & Health* 12, 1, 109–115.

Cohn, M.A., Fredrickson, B.L., Brown, S.L., Mikels, J.A. and Conway, A.M. (2009) 'Happiness unpacked: Positive emotions increase life satisfaction by building resilience.' *Emotion* 9, 3, 361–368.

Csikszentmihalyi, M. (1990) *Flow: The Psychology of Optimal Experience*. New York: HarperCollins Publishers.

Freishtat, A. (2013) The Stress-Exercise Connection: How Does This Work? Orthodox Union. Accessed on 07/03/23 at www.ou.org/life/health/the-stress-exercise-connection-how-does-this-work/

Gerritsen, R.J.S. and Band, G.P.H. (2018) 'Breath of life: The respiratory vagal stimulation model of contemplative activity.' *Frontiers in Human Neuroscience* 12, 397.

Harper, V.J. and Sutton, J.R. (1984) 'Endorphins and exercise.' *Sports Medicine* 1, 2, 154–171.

Kabat-Zinn, J. (1994) *Wherever You Go, There You Are: Mindfulness Meditation in Everyday Life*. New York: Hachette Book Group.

Keng, S.-L., Smoski, M.J. and Robins, C.J. (2011) 'Effects of mindfulness on psychological health: A review of empirical studies.' *Clinical Psychology Review* 31, 6, 1041–1056.

Kirkham, A.J., Breeze, J.M. and Mari-Beffa, P. (2012) 'The impact of verbal instructions on goal-directed behavior.' *Acta Psychologica* 139, 1, 212–219.

Kline, C.E. (2014) 'The bidirectional relationship between exercise and sleep: Implications for exercise adherence and sleep improvement.' *American Journal of Lifestyle Medicine* 8, 6, 375–379.

Lachance, L. and Ramsey, D. (2015) 'Food, mood, and brain health: Implications for the modern clinician.' *The Journal of the Missouri State Medical Association* 112, 2, 111–115.

Leggett, A.N., Zarit, S.H., Kyungmin, K., Almeida, D.M. and Cousino Klein, L. (2015) 'Depressive mood, anger, and daily cortisol of caregivers on high- and low-stress days.' *The Journals of Gerontology: Series B* 70, 6, 820–829.

Lindholm, P. and Lundgren, C.E. (2008). 'The physiology and pathophysiology of human breath-hold diving.' *Journal of Applied Physiology* 106, 284–292.

Linehan, M.M. (2015) *DBT Skills Training Handouts and Worksheets*. New York: The Guilford Press.

May, J.M., Richardi, T.M. and Barth, K.S. (2016) 'Dialectical behavior therapy as treatment for borderline personality disorder.' *The Mental Health Clinician* 6, 2, 62–67.

Mehrabian, A. (1972) *Nonverbal Communication*. New York: Routledge.

Moore, A. (2020) Decoding Body Language: What Do Crossed Arms Actually Mean? MBGMindfulness. Accessed on 07/03/23 at www.mindbodygreen.com/articles/what-do-crossed-arms-mean

Mudyanadzo, T.A., Hauzaree, C., Yerokhina, O., Architha, N.N. and Ashqar, H.M. (2018) 'Irritable bowel syndrome and depression; A shared pathogenesis.' *Cureus* 10, 8, e3178.

Nielsen, J.A., Zielinski, B.A., Ferguson, M.A., Lainhart, J.E. and Anderson, J.S. (2013) 'An evaluation of the left-brain vs. right-brain hypothesis with resting state functional connectivity magnetic resonance imaging.' *PLoS ONE* 8, 8, e71275.

Nummenmaa, L., Glerean, E., Hari, R. and Hietanen, J.K. (2013) 'Bodily maps of emotions.' *Psychological and Cognitive Sciences* 111, 2, 646–651.

Omura, J.D., Brown, D.R., McGuire, L.C., Taylor, C.A. *et al.* (2020) 'Cross-sectional association between physical activity level and subjective cognitive decline among US adults aged ≥45 years, 2015.' *Preventive Medicine* 141, 106279.

Paddock, C. (2017) The Complex Brain Choreography of Split-Second Decisions. Medical News Today. Accessed on 07/03/23 at www.medicalnewstoday.com/articles/320308

Pease, A. (2014) *Body Language*. Uttar Pradesh: Manjul Publishing House Pvt Ltd.

Rees, A., Wiggins, M.W., Helton, W.S., Loveday, T. and O'Hare, D. (2017) 'The impact of breaks on sustained attention in a simulated, semi-automated train control task.' *Applied Cognitive Psychology* 31, 3, 351–359.

Rousay, V. (2021) Bottom-Up Processing: Definition and Examples. Simply Psychology. Accessed on 07/03/23 at www.simplypsychology.org/bottom-up-processing.html

Rubinstein, J.S, Meyer, D.E. and Evans, J.E. (2001) 'Executive control of cognitive processes in task switching.' *Journal of Experimental Psychology: Human Perception and Performance* 27, 4, 763–797.

Scott, A.J., Webb, T.L. and Rowse, G. (2017) 'Does improving sleep lead to better mental health? A protocol for a meta-analytic review of randomised controlled trials.' *British Medical Journal* 7, 9, e016873.

Selye, H. (1950). 'Stress and the general adaptation syndrome.' *British Medical Journal* 1, 1383.

Sharma, A., Madaan, V. and Petty, F.D. (2006) 'Exercise for mental health.' *The Primary Care Companion to the Journal of Clinical Psychiatry* 8, 2, 106.

Strack, F., Martin, L.L. and Stepper, S. (1988) 'Inhibiting and facilitating conditions of the human smile: A nonobtrusive test of the facial feedback hypothesis.' *Journal of Personality and Social Psychology* 54, 5, 768–777.

Van Der Kolk, B. (2014) *The Body Keeps the Score: Brain, Mind, and Body in the Healing of Trauma*. New York: Penguin Books.

Walker, P. (2013) *Complex PTSD: From Surviving to Thriving*. Lafayette: Azure Coyote Publishing.

Westerhof, G.J., Bohlmeijer, E.T. and McAdams, D.P. (2017) 'The relation of ego integrity and despair to personality traits and mental health.' *The Journals of Gerontology: Series B* 72, 3, 400–407.

White, A. (2008) *From Comfort Zone to Performance Management: Understanding Development and Performance.* Baisy-Thy: White & MacLean Publishing.

Zanesco, A.P., King, B.G., MacLean, K.A. and Saron, C.D. (2018) 'Cognitive aging and long-term maintenance of attentional improvements following meditation training.' *Journal of Cognitive Enhancement 2*, 259–275.

Subject Index

Author Index